SIR GAWAIN AND THE GREEN KNIGHT

by the same author

Sir Gawain and the Green Knight

translated by
SIMON ARMITAGE

faber and faber

First published in 2007
by Faber and Faber Limited
Bloomsbury House
74–77 Great Russell Street
London WC1B 3DA
This paperback edition first published in 2009

Typeset in Minion by Faber and Faber Limited
Printed in England by T. J. International Ltd, Padstow, Cornwall

A CIP record for this book
is available from the British Library

ISBN 978-0-571-22328-2

21

Introduction

We know next to nothing about the author of the poem which has come to be called *Sir Gawain and the Green Knight*. It was probably written around 1400. In the early seventeenth century the manuscript was recorded as belonging to a Yorkshireman, Henry Saville of Bank. It was later acquired by Sir Robert Cotton, whose collection also included the Lindisfarne Gospels and the only surviving manuscript of *Beowulf*. The poem then lay dormant for over two hundred years, not coming to light until Queen Victoria was on the throne, thus leapfrogging the attentions of some of our greatest writers and critics. The manuscript, a small, unprepossessing thing, would fit comfortably into an average-size hand, were anyone actually allowed to touch it. Now referred to as Cotton Nero A.x., it is considered not only a most brilliant example of Middle English poetry but one of the jewels in the crown of English Literature, and sits in the British Library under conditions of high security and controlled humidity.

To cast eyes on the manuscript, or even to shuffle the unbound pages of the Early English Text Society's facsimile edition, is to be intrigued by the handwriting: stern, stylish letters, like crusading chess pieces, fall into orderly ranks along faintly ruled lines. But the man whose calligraphy we ponder, a jobbing scribe probably, was not the author. The person who has become known as the Gawain poet remains as shadowy as the pages themselves. Among many other reasons, it is partly this anonymity which has made the poem so attractive to latter-day translators. The lack of authorship seems to serve as an invitation, opening up a space within the poem for a new writer to occupy. Its comparatively recent rediscovery acts as a further draw; if Milton or Pope had put their stamp on it, or if Dr Johnson had offered an opinion, or if Keats or Coleridge or

Wordsworth had drawn it into their orbit, such an invitation might now appear less forthcoming.

The diction of the original tells us that its author was, broadly speaking, a northerner. Or we could say a midlander. The linguistic epicentre of the poem has been located in the area of the Cheshire-Staffordshire-Derbyshire border. Some researchers claim to have identified Swythamley Grange as the Castle of Hautdesert, or the jagged peaks of The Roaches as those 'rogh knokled knarres with knorned stones' (2166). Lud's Church, a natural fissure in the rocks near the village of Flash, in Derbyshire, has been proposed as the site of the Green Chapel. 'Hit had a hole on the ende and on ayther syde,/ And overgrowen with gres in glodes aywhere,/ And all was holw inwith, nobot an olde cave/ Or a crevisse of an olde cragge' (2180–4). It may or may not be the place, but to stand in that mossy cleft which cannot have changed much over the centuries is to believe that the author had an actual landscape in mind when he conceived the poem, and lured his young protagonist into a northern region to legitimize his vocabulary and to make good use of his surrounding geography. A similar strategy has informed this translation; although my own part of northern England is separated from Lud's Church by the swollen uplands of the Peak District, coaxing Gawain and his poem back into the Pennines was always part of the plan.

Of course to the trained medievalist the poem is perfectly readable in its original form; no translation necessary. And even for the non-specialist, certain lines, such as, 'Bot Arthure wolde not ete til all were served' (85), especially when placed within the context of the narrative, present little problem. Conversely, lines such as 'Forthy, iwis, bi your wille, wende me behoves' (1065) are incomprehensible to the general reader. But it is the lines which fall somewhere between those extremes – the majority of lines, in fact – which fascinate the most. They seem to make sense, though not quite. To the untrained eye, it is as if the poem is lying beneath a thin coat of ice, tantalizingly near yet frustratingly blurred. To a contemporary poet, one interested in narrative and form, and to a northerner who not only recognizes plenty of the poem's dialect but who detects an echo of his own speech rhythms within the original, the urge to blow a little warm breath across that layer of frosting eventually proved irresistible.

Not all poems are stories, but *Sir Gawain and the Green Knight* most certainly is. After briefly anchoring its historical credentials in the siege of Troy, the poem quickly delivers us into Arthurian Britain, at Christmas time, with the knights of the Round Table in good humour and full voice. But the festivities at Camelot are to be disrupted by the astonishing appearance of a green knight. Not just a knight wearing green clothes, but a weird being whose skin and hair is green, and whose horse is green as well. The gatecrasher lays down a seemingly absurd challenge, involving beheading and revenge. Alert to the opportunity, a young knight, Gawain, Arthur's nephew, rises from the table. What follows is a test of courage and a test of his heart, and during the ensuing episodes, which span an entire calendar year, Gawain must steel himself against fear and temptation. The poem is also a ghost story, a thriller, a romance, an adventure story and a morality tale. For want of a better word, it is also a myth, and like all great myths of the past its meanings seem to have adapted and evolved, proving itself eerily relevant six hundred years later. As one example, certain aspects Gawain's situation seem oddly redolent of a more contemporary predicament, namely our complex and delicate relationship with the natural world. The Gawain poet had never heard of climate change and was not a prophet anticipating the onset of global warming. But medieval society lived hand in hand with nature, and nature was as much an enemy as a friend. It is not just for decoration that the poem includes passages relating to the turning of the seasons, or detailed accounts of the landscape, or graphic descriptions of our dealings with the animal kingdom. The knight who throws down the challenge at

Camelot is both ghostly and real. Supernatural, yes, but also flesh and blood. He is something in the likeness of ourselves, and he is not purple or orange or blue with yellow stripes. Gawain must negotiate a deal with a man who wears the colours of the leaves and the fields. He must strike an honest bargain with this manifestation of nature, and his future depends on it.

Over the years there have been dozens, possibly hundreds of translations of *Sir Gawain and the Green Knight*, ranging from important scholarly restorations, to free-handed poetic or prose versions, to exercises in form and technique by students of Middle English, many of them posted on the internet. Some translators, for perfectly valid reasons and with great success, have chosen not to imitate its highly alliterative form. But to me, alliteration is the warp and weft of the poem, without which it is just so many fine threads. In some very elemental way, the story and the sense of the poem is directly located within its sound. The percussive patterning of the words serves to reinforce their meaning and to countersink them within the memory. So in trying to harmonize with the original rather than transcribe every last word of it, certain liberties have been taken. This is not an exercise in linguistic forensics or medieval history; the intention has always been to produce a living, inclusive and readable piece of work in its own right. In other words, the amibtion has been *poetry*.

On the subject of alliteration, it should be mentioned that within each line it is the *stressed* syllables which count. A line like 'and retrieves the intestines in time-honoured style' (1612) might appear not to alliterate at first glance. But read it out loud, and the repetition of that 't' sound – the tut-tutting, the spit of revulsion, the squirming of the warm, wet tongue as it makes contacts the roof of the mouth – seems to suggest a physical relationship with the action being described. If the technique is effective, as well as understanding what we are being told we take a step closer to actually experiencing it. It is an attempt to combine meaning with feeling. This is a translation not only for the eye, but for the ear and the voice as well.

Sir Gawain and the Green Knight is a poem which succeeds through a series of vivid contrasts: standard English contrasting with colloquial speech; the devotion and virtue of the young knight contrasting with the growling blood-lust of his green foe; exchanges of courtly love contrasting with none-too-subtle sexual innuendo; exquisite robes and priceless crowns contrasting with spurting blood and the steaming organs of butchered deer; polite, indoor society contrasting with the untamed, unpredictable outdoors . . . and so on. Those contrasts stretch the imaginative universe of the poem and make it three-dimensional. Without the space they open up, there would be no poem to speak of. The same contrasts can be observed in the form of the poem as well as its tone, with elements of order and disorder at work throughout, often operating simultaneously. On the side of order we have the four-beat pulse of each line, the very particular number of verses, and the rhyme and rhythm of the 'bob and wheel' sections. On the side of disorder we have the unequal line lengths, the variable verse lengths, and the wildly fluctuating pace of the story. Even the alliteration, constant and insistent for the most part, occasionally fades from view altogether. So within the strictures and confines of this very formal piece we detect a human presence, the Gawain poet, a disciplined craftsman who also liked to run risks and take liberties. He would appear to have set himself a series of rules, then consciously and conspicuously gone about bending them. As his translator, I hope to have been guided by his example.

Simon Armitage

Sir Gawain and the Green Knight

FITT I

Once the siege and assault of Troy had ceased,
with the city a smoke-heap of cinders and ash,
the turncoat whose tongue had tricked his own men
was tried for his treason – the truest crime on earth.
Then noble Aeneas and his noble lords
went conquering abroad, laying claim to the crowns
of the wealthiest kingdoms in the western world.
Mighty Romulus quickly careered towards Rome
and conceived a city in magnificent style
which from then until now has been known by his name.   10
Ticius constructed townships in Tuscany
and Langobard did likewise, building homes in Lombardy.
And further afield, over the Sea of France,
on Britain's broad hill-tops, Felix Brutus made
                    his stand.
          And wonder, dread and war
          have lingered in that land
          where loss and love in turn
          have held the upper hand.

After Britain was built by this founding father
        a bold race bred there, battle-happy men
        causing trouble and torment in turbulent times,
        and through history more strangeness has happened here
        than anywhere else I know of on Earth.
        But most regal of rulers in the royal line
        was Arthur, who I heard is honoured above all,
        and the inspiring story I intend to spin
        has moved the hearts and minds of many –
        an awesome episode in the legends of Arthur.
So listen a little while to my tale if you will
        and I'll tell it as it's told in the town where it trips from
                        the tongue;
                and as it has been inked
                in stories bold and strong,
                through letters which, once linked,
                have lasted loud and long.

It was Christmas at Camelot – King Arthur's court,
where the great and the good of the land had gathered,
all the righteous lords of the ranks of the Round Table
quite properly carousing and revelling in pleasure.   40
Time after time, in tournaments of joust,
they had lunged at each other with levelled lances
then returned to the castle to carry on their carolling,
for the feasting lasted a full fortnight and one day,
with more food and drink than a fellow could dream of.
The hubbub of their humour was heavenly to hear:
pleasant dialogue by day and dancing after dusk,
so the house and its hall were lit with happiness
and lords and ladies were luminous with joy.
Such a coming together of the gracious and the glad: 50
the most chivalrous and courteous knights known in Christendom;
the most wonderful women to have walked in this world;
the handsomest king to be crowned at court.
Fine folk with their futures before them, there in
                    that hall.
          Their highly honoured king
          was happiest of all:
          no nobler knights had come
          within a castle's wall.

60 With New Year so young it still yawned and stretched
helpings were doubled on the dais that day.
And as king and company were coming to the hall
the choir in the chapel fell suddenly quiet,
then a chorus erupted from the courtiers and clerks:
'Noel,' they cheered, then 'Noel, Noel.'
'New Year Gifts!' the knights cried next
as they pressed forward to offer their presents,
teasing with frivolous favours and forfeits,
till those ladies who lost couldn't help but laugh,
70 and the undefeated were far from forlorn.
Their merrymaking rolled on in this manner until mealtime,
when, washed and worthy, they went to the table,
and were seated in order of honour, as was apt,
with Guinevere in their gathering, gloriously framed
at her place on the platform, pricelessly curtained
by silk to each side, and canopied across
with French weave and fine tapestry from the far east
studded with stones and stunning gems.
Pearls beyond pocket. Pearls beyond purchase
80   or price.
            But not one stone outshone
            the quartz of the queen's eyes;
            with hand on heart, no one
            could argue otherwise.

But Arthur would not eat until all were served.
He brimmed with ebullience, being almost boyish
in his love of life, and what he liked the least
was to sit still watching the seasons slip by.
His blood was busy and he buzzed with thoughts,
and the matter which played on his mind at that moment   90
was his pledge to take no portion from his plate
on such a special day until a story was told:
some far-fetched yarn or outrageous fable,
the tallest of tales, yet one ringing with truth,
like the action-packed epics of men-at-arms.
Or till some chancer had challenged his chosen knight,
dared him, with a lance, to lay life on the line,
to stare death face to face and accept defeat
should fortune or fate smile more favourably on his foe.
Within Camelot's castle this was the custom,   100
at feasts and festivals when the fellowship
                    would meet.
            With features proud and fine
            he stood there tall and straight,
            a king at Christmas time
            amid great merriment.

And still he stands there just being himself,
chatting away charmingly, exchanging views.
Good Sir Gawain is seated by Guinevere,
and at Arthur's other side sits Agravain the Hard Hand,
both nephews of the king and notable knights.
At the head sat Bishop Baldwin as Arthur's guest of honour,
with Ywain, son of Urien, to eat beside him.
And as soon as the nobles had sampled the spread
the stalwarts on the benches to both sides were served.
The first course comes in to the fanfare and clamour
of blasting trumpets hung with trembling banners,
then pounding double-drums and dinning pipes,
weird sounds and wails of such warbled wildness
that to hear and feel them made the heart float free.
Flavoursome delicacies of flesh were fetched in
and the freshest of foods, so many in fact
there was scarcely space to present the stews
or to set the soups in the silver bowls on
                    the cloth.
            Each guest received his share
            of bread or meat or broth;
            a dozen plates per pair –
            plus beer or wine, or both!

Now, on the subject of supper I'll say no more   130
as it's obvious to everyone that no one went without.
Because another sound, a new sound, suddenly drew near,
which might signal the king to sample his supper,
for barely had the horns finished blowing their breath
and with starters just spooned to the seated guests,
a fearful form appeared, framed in the door:
a mountain of a man, immeasurably high,
a hulk of a human from head to hips,
so long and thick in his loins and his limbs
I should genuinely judge him to be a half-giant,   140
or a most massive man, the mightiest of mortals.
But handsome too, like any horseman worth his horse,
for despite the bulk and brawn of his body
his stomach and waist were slender and sleek.
In fact in all features he was finely formed
                    it seemed.
          Amazement seized their minds,
          no soul had ever seen
          a knight of such a kind –
          entirely emerald green.   150

And his gear and garments were green as well:
a tight-fitting tunic, tailored to his torso,
and a cloak to cover him, the cloth fully lined
with smoothly shorn fur clearly showing, and faced
with all-white ermine, as was the hood,
worn shawled on his shoulders, shucked from his head.
On his lower limbs his leggings were also green,
wrapped closely round his calves, and his sparkling spurs
were green-gold, strapped with stripy silk,
160 and were set on his stockings, for this stranger was shoeless.
In all vestments he revealed himself veritably verdant!
From his belt-hooks and buckle to the baubles and gems
arrayed so richly around his costume
and adorning the saddle, stitched onto silk.
All the details of his dress are difficult to describe,
embroidered as it was with butterflies and birds,
green beads emblazoned on a background of gold.
All the horse's tack – harness-strap, hind-strap,
the eye of the bit, each alloy and enamel
170 and the stirrups he stood in – were similarly tinted,
and the same with the cantle and the skirts of the saddle,
all glimmering and glinting with the greenest jewels.
And the horse: every hair was green, from hoof
       to mane.
    A steed of pure green stock.
    Each snort and shudder strained
    the hand-stitched bridle, but
    his rider had him reined.

The fellow in green was in fine fettle.
The hair of his head was as green as his horse,   180
fine flowing locks which fanned across his back,
plus a bushy green beard growing down to his breast,
and his face-hair along with the hair of his head
was lopped in a line at elbow-length
so half his arms were gowned in green growth,
crimped at the collar, like a king's cape.
The mane of his mount was groomed to match,
combed and knotted into curlicues
then tinselled with gold, tied and twisted
green over gold, green over gold . . .   190
The fetlocks were finished in the same fashion
with bright green ribbon braided with beads,
as was the tail – to its tippety-tip!
And a long, tied thong lacing it tight
was strung with gold bells which resounded and shone.
No waking man had witnessed such a warrior
or weird war-horse – otherworldly, yet flesh
                    and bone.
          A look of lightning flashed
          from somewhere in his soul.   200
          The force of that man's fist
          would be a thunderbolt.

Yet he wore no helmet and no hauberk either,
no armoured apparel or plate was apparent,
and he swung no sword nor sported any shield,
but held in one hand a sprig of holly –
of all the evergreens the greenest ever –
and in the other hand held the mother of all axes,
a cruel piece of kit I kid you not:
210 the head was an ell in length at least
and forged in green steel with a gilt finish;
the skull-busting blade was so stropped and buffed
it could shear a man's scalp and shave him to boot.
The handle which fitted that fiend's great fist
was inlaid with iron, end to end,
with green pigment picking out impressive designs.
From stock to neck, where it stopped with a knot,
a lace was looped the length of the haft,
trimmed with tassels and tails of string
220 fastened firmly in place by forest-green buttons.
And he kicks on, canters through that crowded hall
towards the top table, not the least bit timid,
cocksure of himself, sitting high in the saddle.
'And who,' he bellows, without breaking breath,
'is governor of this gaggle? I'll be glad to know.
It's with him and him alone that I'll have
        my say.'
        The green man steered his gaze
        deep into every eye,
230   explored each person's face
        to probe for a reply.

The guests looked on. They gaped and they gawked
and were mute with amazement: what did it mean
that human and horse could develop this hue,
should grow to be grass-green or greener still,
like green enamel emboldened by bright gold?
Some stood and stared then stepped a little closer,
drawn near to the knight to know his next move;
they'd seen some sights, but this was something special,
a miracle or magic, or so they imagined.   240
Yet several of the lords were like statues in their seats,
left speechless and rigid, not risking a response.
The hall fell hushed, as if all who were present
had slipped into sleep or some trance-like state.
                    No doubt
            not all were stunned and stilled
            by dread, but duty-bound
            to hold their tongues until
            their sovereign could respond.

250 Then the king acknowledged this curious occurrence,
cordially addressed him, keeping his cool.
'A warm welcome, sir, this winter's night.
My name is Arthur, I am head of this house.
Won't you slide from that saddle and stay a while,
and the business which brings you we shall learn of later.'
'No,' said the knight, 'it's not in my nature
to idle or allack about this evening.
But because your acclaim is so loudly chorused,
and your castle and brotherhood are called the best,
260 the strongest men ever to mount the saddle,
the worthiest knights ever known to the world,
both in competition and true combat,
and since courtesy, so it's said, is championed here,
I'm intrigued, and attracted to your door at this time.
Be assured by this hollin stem here in my hand
that I mean no menace. So expect no malice,
for if I'd slogged here tonight to slay and slaughter
my helmet and hauberk wouldn't be at home
and my sword and spear would be here at my side,
270 and more weapons of war, as I'm sure you're aware.
I'm clothed for peace, not kitted out for conflict.
But if you're half as honourable as I've heard folk say
you'll gracefully grant me this game which I ask for
                    by right.'
            Then Arthur answered, 'Knight
            most courteous, you claim
            a fair, unarmoured fight.
            We'll see you have the same.'

'I'm spoiling for no scrap, I swear. Besides,
the bodies on these benches are just bum-fluffed bairns.   280
If I'd ridden to your castle rigged out for a ruck
these lightweight adolescents wouldn't last a minute.
But it's Yuletide – a time of youthfulness, yes?
So at Christmas in this court I lay down a challenge:
if a person here present, within these premises,
is big or bold or red-blooded enough
to strike me one stroke and be struck in return,
I shall give him as a gift this gigantic cleaver
and the axe shall be his to handle how he likes.
I'll kneel, bare my neck and take the first knock.   290
So who has the gall? The gumption? The guts?
Who'll spring from his seat and snatch this weapon?
I offer the axe – who'll have it as his own?
I'll afford one free hit from which I won't flinch,
and promise that twelve months will pass in peace,
                then claim
            the duty I deserve
            in one year and one day.
            Does no one have the nerve
            to wager in this way?'   300

Flustered at first, now totally foxed
were the household and the lords, both the highborn and the low.
Still stirruped, the knight swivelled round in his saddle
looking left and right, his red eyes rolling
beneath the bristles of his bushy green brows,
his beard swishing from side to side.
When the court kept its counsel he cleared his throat
and stiffened his spine. Then he spoke his mind:
'So here is the House of Arthur,' he scoffed,
310   'whose virtues reverberate across vast realms.
Where's the fortitude and fearlessness you're so famous for?
And the breathtaking bravery and the big-mouth bragging?
The towering reputation of the Round Table,
skittled and scuppered by a stranger – what a scandal!
You flap and you flinch and I've not raised a finger!'
Then he laughed so loud that their leader saw red.
Blood flowed to his fine-featured face and he raged
                inside.
      His men were also hurt –
320   those words had pricked their pride.
      But born so brave at heart
      the king stepped up one stride.

'Your request,' he countered, 'is quite insane,
and folly finds the man who flirts with the fool.
No warrior worth his salt would be worried by your words,
so in heaven's good name hand over the axe
and I'll happily fulfil the favour you ask.'
He strides to him swiftly and seizes his arm;
the man-mountain dismounts in one mighty leap.
Then Arthur grips the axe, grabs it by its haft   330
and takes it above him, intending to attack.
Yet the stranger before him stands up straight,
highest in the house by at least a head.
Quite simply he stands there stroking his beard,
fiddling with his coat, his face without fear,
about to be bludgeoned, but no more bothered
than a guest at the table being given a goblet
                    of wine.
            By Guinevere, Gawain
            now to his king inclines   340
            and says, 'I stake my claim.
            This moment must be mine.'

'Should you call me, courteous lord,' said Gawain to his king,
'to rise from my seat and stand at your side,
politely take leave of my place at the table
and quit without causing offence to my queen,
then I shall come to your counsel before this great court.
For I find it unfitting, as my fellow knights would,
when a deed of such daring is dangled before us
350   that you take on this trial – tempted as you are –
when brave, bold men are seated on these benches,
men never matched in the mettle of their minds,
never beaten or bettered in the field of battle.
I am weakest of your warriors and feeblest of wit;
loss of my life would be grieved the least.
Were I not your nephew my life would mean nothing;
to be born of your blood is my body's only claim.
Such a foolish affair is unfitting for a king,
so, being first to come forward, it should fall to me.
360   And if my proposal is improper, let no other person
                    stand blame.'
                The knighthood then unites
                and each knight says the same:
                their king can stand aside
                and give Gawain the game.

So the sovereign instructed his knight to stand.
Getting to his feet he moved graciously forward
and knelt before Arthur, taking hold of the axe.
Letting go of it, Arthur then held up his hand
to give young Gawain the blessing of God   370
and hope he finds firmness in heart and fist.
'Take care, young cousin, to catch him cleanly.
Use full-blooded force, then you needn't fear
the blow which he threatens to trade in return.'
Gawain, with the weapon, walked towards the warrior,
and they stand face to face, not one man afraid.
Then the green knight spoke, growled at Gawain,
'Before we compete, repeat what we've promised.
And start by saying your name to me, sir,
and tell me the truth so I can take it on trust.'   380
'In good faith, it's Gawain,' said the God-fearing knight,
'I heave this axe, and whatever happens after,
in twelvemonth's time I'll be struck in return
with any weapon you wish, and by you and you
                        alone.'
            The other answers, says
            'Well, by my living bones,
            I welcome you, Gawain,
            to bring the blade-head home.'

390 'Gawain,' said the green knight, 'By God, I'm glad
the favour I've called for will fall from your fist.
You've perfectly repeated the promise we've made
and the terms of the contest are crystal clear.
Except for one thing: you must solemnly swear
that you'll seek me yourself; that you'll search me out
to the ends of the earth to earn the same blow
as you'll dole out today in this decorous hall.'
'But where will you be? Where's your abode?
You're a man of mystery, as God is my maker.
400 Which court do you come from and what are you called?
There is knowledge I need, including your name,
then by wit I'll work out the way to your door
and keep to our contract, so cross my heart.'
'But enough at New Year. It needs nothing more,'
said the war-man in green to worthy Gawain.
'I could tell you the truth once you've taken the blow;
if you smite me smartly I could spell out the facts
of my house and home and my name, if it helps,
then you'll pay me a visit and vouch for our pact.
410 Or if I keep quiet you might cope much better,
loafing and lounging here, looking no further. But
                    you stall!
          Now grasp that gruesome axe
          and show your striking style.'
          He answered, 'Since you ask,'
          and touched the tempered steel.

In the standing position he prepared to be struck,
bent forward, revealing a flash of green flesh
as he heaped his hair to the crown of his head,
the nape of his neck now naked and ready.   420
Gawain grips the axe and heaves it heavenwards,
plants his left foot firmly on the floor in front,
then swings it swiftly towards the bare skin.
The cleanness of the strike cleaved the spinal cord
and parted the fat and the flesh so far
that that bright steel blade took a bite from the floor.
The handsome head tumbles onto the earth
and the king's men kick it as it clatters past.
Blood gutters brightly against his green gown,
yet the man doesn't shudder or stagger or sink   430
but trudges towards them on those tree-trunk legs
and rummages around, reaches at their feet
and cops hold of his head and hoists it high,
and strides to his steed, snatches the bridle,
steps into the stirrup and swings into the saddle
still gripping his head by a handful of hair.
Then he settles himself in his seat with the ease
of a man unmarked, never mind being minus
                    his head!
          And when he wheeled about   440
          his bloody neck still bled.
          His point was proved. The court
          was deadened now with dread.

For that scalp and skull now swung from his fist;
towards the top table he turned the face
and it opened its eyelids, stared straight ahead
and spoke this speech, which you'll hear for yourselves:
'Sir Gawain, be wise enough to keep your word
and faithfully follow me until I'm found
450 as you vowed in this hall within hearing of these horsemen.
You're charged with getting to the green chapel,
to reap what you've sown. You'll rightfully receive
the justice you are due just as January dawns.
Men know my name as the green chapel knight
and even a fool couldn't fail to find me.
So come, or be called a coward for ever.'
With a tug of the reins he twisted around
and, head still in hand, galloped out of the hall,
so the hooves brought fire from the flame in the flint.
460 Which kingdom he came from they hadn't a clue,
no more than they knew where he made for next.
                    And then?
               Well, with the green man gone
               they laughed and grinned again.
               And yet such goings on
               were magic to those men.

And although King Arthur was awe-struck at heart
no sign of it showed. Instead he spoke
to his queen of queens with courteous words:
'Dear lady, don't be daunted by this deed today,   470
it's in keeping that such strangeness should occur at Christmas
between sessions of banter and seasonal song,
amid the lively pastimes of ladies and lords.
And at least I'm allowed to eat at last,
having witnessed such wonder, wouldn't you say?'
Then he glanced at Gawain and was graceful with his words:
'Now hang up your axe – one hack is enough.'
So it dangled from the drape behind the dais
so that men who saw it would be mesmerised and amazed,
and give voice, on its evidence, to that stunning event.   480
Then the two of them turned and walked to the table,
the monarch and his man, and were met with food –
double dishes apiece, rare delicacies,
all manner of meals – and the music of minstrels.
And they danced and sang till the sun went down
                        that day.
            But mind your mood, Gawain,
            keep blacker thoughts at bay,
            or lose this lethal game
            you've promised you will play.   490

FITT II

This happening was a gift – just as Arthur had asked for
and had yearned to hear of while the year was young.
And if guests had no subject as they strolled to their seats,
now they chattered of Gawain's chances in this challenge.
And Gawain had been glad to begin the game,
but don't be shocked if the plot turns pear-shaped:
for men might be merry when addled with mead
but each year, short-lived, is unlike the last
and rarely resolves in the style it arrived.
So the festival finishes and a new year follows   500
in eternal sequence, season by season.
After lavish Christmas come the lean days of Lent
when the flesh is tested with fish and simple food.
Then the world's weather wages war on winter:
cold shrinks earthwards and clouds climb;
sun-warmed, shimmering rain comes showering
onto meadows and fields where flowers unfurl,
and woods and grounds wear a wardrobe of green.
Birds burble with life and build busily
as summer spreads, settling on slopes as   510
                    it should.
            Now every hedgerow brims
            with blossom and with bud,
            and lively songbirds sing
            from lovely, leafy woods.

So summer comes in season with its subtle airs,
when the west wind sighs among shoots and seeds,
and those plants which flower and flourish are a pleasure
as their leaves let drip their drink of dew
520 and they sparkle and glitter when glanced by sunlight.
Then autumn arrives to harden the harvest
and with it comes a warning to ripen before winter.
The drying airs arrive, driving up dust
from the face of the earth to the heights of heaven,
and wild sky wrestles the sun with its winds,
and the leaves of the lime lay littered on the ground,
and grass that was green turns withered and grey.
Then all which had risen over-ripens and rots
and yesterday on yesterday the year dies away,
530 and winter returns, as is the way of the world
                    through time.
            At Michaelmas the moon
            stands like that season's sign,
            a warning to Gawain
            to rouse himself and ride.

Yet by All Saints' Day he was still at Arthur's side,
and they feasted in the name of their noble knight
with the revels and riches of the Round Table.
The lords of that hall and their loving ladies
were sad and concerned for the sake of their knight,   540
but nevertheless they made light of his load.
Men joyless at his plight made jokes and rejoiced.
Then sorrowfully, after supper, he spoke with his uncle,
and openly talked of the trip he must take:
'Now, lord of my life, I must ask for your leave.
You were witness to my wager. I have no wish
to re-tell you the terms – they're nothing but a trifle.
I must set out tomorrow to receive that stroke
from the knight in green, and let God be my guide.'
Then the cream of Camelot crowded around: 550
Ywain and Eric and others of that ilk,
Sir Dodinal the Dreaded, the Duke of Clarence,
Lancelot, Lionel, Lucan the Good,
and Sir Bors and Sir Bedevere – both big names,
and powerful men such as Mador de la Port.
This courtly committee approaches the king
to offer up heartfelt advice to our hero.
And sounds of sadness and sorrow were heard
that one as worthy and well-liked as Gawain
should suffer that strike but offer no stroke in   560
            reply.
        Yet keeping calm the knight
        just quipped, 'Why should I shy
        away? If fate is kind
        or cruel man still must try.'

He remained all that day and in the morning he dressed,
asked early for his arms and all were produced.
First a rug of rare cloth was unrolled on the floor,
heaped with gear which glimmered and gleamed,
570 and onto it he stepped to receive his armoured suit.
He tries on his tunic of extravagant silk,
then the neatly cut cloak, closed at the neck,
its lining finished with a layer of white fur.
Then they settled his feet into steel shoes
and clad his calves, clamped them with greaves,
then hinged and highly polished plates
were knotted with gold thread to the knight's knees.
Then leg-guards were fitted, lagging the flesh,
attached with thongs to his thick-set thighs.
580 Then comes the suit of shimmering steel rings
encasing his body and his costly clothes:
well burnished braces to both of his arms,
good elbow guards and glinting metal gloves,
all the trimmings and trappings of a knight tricked out
                    to ride:
            a metal suit that shone;
            gold spurs which gleam with pride;
            a keen sword swinging from
            the silk belt to his side.

Fastened in his armour he seemed fabulous, famous,   590
every link looking golden to the very last loop.
Yet for all that metal he still made it to Mass,
honoured the Almighty before the high altar.
After which he comes to the king and his consorts
and asks to take leave of the ladies and lords;
they escort and kiss him and commend him to Christ.
Now Gringolet is rigged out and ready to ride
with a saddle which flickered with fine gold fringes
and was set with new studs for the special occasion.
The bridle was bound with stripes of bright gold,   600
the apparel of the panels was matched in appearance
to the colour of the saddle-bows and cropper and cover,
and nails of red gold were arrayed all around,
shining splendidly like splintered sunlight.
Then he holds up his helmet and kisses it without haste;
it was strongly stapled and its lining was stuffed,
and sat high on his head, fastened behind
with a colourful cloth to cover his neck
embroidered and bejewelled with brilliant gems
on the broad silk border, and with birds on the seams   610
such as painted parrots perched among periwinkles
and turtle doves and true-love-knots, tightly entwined
as if women had worked at it seven winters
                    at least.
          The diamond diadem
          was greater still. It gleamed
          with flawless, flashing gems
          both clear and smoked, it seemed.

Then they showed him the shining scarlet shield
620   with its pentangle painted in pure gold.
He seized it by its strap and slung it round his neck;
he looked well in what he wore, and was worthy of it.
And why the pentangle was appropriate to that prince
I intend to say, though it will stall our story.
It is a symbol that Solomon once set in place
and is taken to this day as a token of fidelity,
for the form of the figure is a five-pointed star
and each line overlaps and links with the last
so is ever-eternal, and when spoken of in England
630   is known by the name of the endless knot.
So it suits this soldier in his spotless armour,
fully faithful in five ways five times over.
For Gawain was as good as the purest gold –
devoid of vices but virtuous, loyal
           and kind,
      so bore that badge on both
      his shawl and shield alike.
      A prince who talked the truth.
      A notable. A knight.

First he was deemed flawless in his five senses; 640
and secondly his five fingers were never at fault;
and thirdly his faith was founded in the five wounds
Christ received on the cross, as the creed recalls.
And fourthly, if that soldier struggled in skirmish
one thought pulled him through above all other things:
the fortitude he found in the five joys
which Mary had conceived in her son, our Saviour.
For precisely that reason the princely rider
had the shape of her image inside his shield,
so by catching her eye his courage would not crack. 650
The fifth set of five which I heard the knight followed
included friendship and fraternity with fellow men,
purity and politeness that impressed at all times,
and pity, which surpassed all pointedness. Five things
which meant more to Gawain than to most other men.
So these five sets of five were fixed in this knight,
each linked to the last through the endless line,
a five-pointed form which never failed,
never stronger to one side or slack at the other,
but unbroken in its being from beginning to end 660
however its trail is tracked and traced.
So the star on the spangling shield he sported
shone royally, in gold, on a ruby-red background,
the pure pentangle as people have called it
            for years.
        Then, lance in hand, held high,
        and got up in his gear
        he bids them all goodbye
        one final time, he fears.

670   Spiked with the spurs the steed sped away
with such force that the fire-stones sparked underfoot.
All sighed at the sight, and with sinking hearts
they whispered their worries to one another,
concerned for their comrade. 'A pity, by Christ,
if a lord so noble should lose his life.
To find his equal on earth would be far from easy.
Cleverer to have acted with caution and care,
deemed him a duke – a title he was due –
a leader of men, lord of many lands;
680   better that than being battered into oblivion,
beheaded by an ogre through headstrong pride.
How unknown for a king to take counsel of a knight
in the grip of an engrossing Christmas game.'
Warm tears welled up in their weepy eyes
as gallant Sir Gawain galloped from court
             that day.
        He sped from home and hearth
        and went his winding way
        on steep and snaking paths,
690   just as the story says.

Now through England's realm he rides and rides,
Sir Gawain, God's servant, on his grim quest,
passing long dark nights unloved and alone,
foraging to feed, finding little to call food,
with no friend but his horse through forests and hills
and only our Lord in heaven to hear him.
He wanders near to the north of Wales
with the Isles of Anglesey off to the left.
He keeps to the coast, fording each course,
crossing at Holy Head and coming ashore   700
in the wilds of the Wirral, whose wayward people
both God and good men have quite given up on.
And he constantly enquires of those he encounters
if they know, or not, in this neck of the woods,
of a great green man or a green chapel.
No, they say, never. Never in their lives.
They know of neither a knight nor a chapel

          so strange.
       He trails through bleak terrain.
       His mood and manner change   710
       at every twist and turn
       towards that chosen church.

In a strange region he scales steep slopes;
far from his friends he cuts a lonely figure.
Where he bridges a brook or wades through a waterway
ill fortune brings him face to face with a foe
so foul or fierce he is bound to use force.
So momentous are his travels among the mountains
to tell just a tenth would be a tall order.
720   Here he scraps with serpents and snarling wolves,
here he tangles with wodwos causing trouble in the crags,
or with bulls and bears and the odd wild boar.
Hard on his heels through the highlands come giants.
Only diligence and faith in the face of death
will keep him from becoming a corpse or carrion.
And the wars were one thing, but winter was worse:
clouds shed their cargo of crystallized rain
which froze as it fell to the frost-glazed earth.
With nerves frozen numb he napped in his armour,
730   bivouacked in the blackness amongst bare rocks
where melt-water streamed from the snow-capped summits
and high overhead hung chandeliers of ice.
So in peril and pain Sir Gawain made progress,
criss-crossing the countryside until Christmas

                Eve. Then
        at that time of tiding,
        he prayed to highest heaven.
        Let Mother Mary guide him
        towards some house or haven.

Next morning he moves on, skirts the mountainside,   740
descends a deep forest, densely overgrown,
with ancient oaks in huddles of hundreds
and vaulting hills above each half of the valley.
Hazel and hawthorn are interwoven,
decked and draped in damp, shaggy moss,
and bedraggled birds on bare, black branches
pipe pitifully into the piercing cold.
Under cover of the canopy he girded Gringolet
though mud and marshland, a most mournful man,
concerned and afraid in case he should fail   750
in the worship of our Deity, who, on that date
was born the Virgin's son to save our souls.
He prayed with heavy heart: 'Father, hear me,
and Lady Mary, our mother most mild,
let me happen on some house where mass might be heard,
and matins in the morning; meekly I ask –
and here I utter my pater, ave
                  and creed.
            He rides the path and prays,
            dismayed by his misdeeds,
            and signs Christ's cross and says,   760
            'Be near me in my need.'

No sooner had he signed himself three times
than he became aware, in those woods, of high walls
in a moat, on a mound, bordered by the boughs
of thick-trunked timber which trimmed the water.
The most commanding castle a knight ever kept,
positioned on a site of sweeping parkland
with a palisade of pikes pitched in the earth
in the midst of tall trees for two miles or more.
From the corner of his eye this castle became clearer
as it sparkled and shone within shimmering oaks,
and with helmet in hand he offered up thanks
to Jesus and Saint Julian, both gentle and good,
who had courteously heard him and heeded his cry.
'A lodging at last. So allow it, my Lord.'
Then he girded Gringolet with his gilded spurs,
and purely by chance chose the principal approach
to the building, which brought him to the end of the bridge
in haste.
        The drawbridge stood withdrawn,
        the front gates were shut fast.
        Such well-constructed walls
        would blunt the storm-wind's blast.

In the saddle of his steed he halts on the slope
of the delving moat with its double ditch.
Out of water of wondrous depth, the walls
then loomed overhead to a heavenly height,
course after course of crafted stone,
then battlements embellished in the boldest style   790
and turrets arranged around the ramparts
with lockable loopholes set into the lookouts.
The knight had not seen a more stunning structure.
Further in, his eye was drawn to a hall
attended, architecturally, by many tall towers
with a series of spires spiking the air
all crowned by carvings exquisitely cut.
Uncountable chimneys the colour of chalk
sprutted from the roof and sparkled in the sun.
So perfect was that vision of painted pinnacles   800
clustered within the castle's enclosure
it appeared that the place was cut from paper.
Then a notion occurred to that noble knight:
to inveigle a visit, get invited inside,
to be hosted and housed, and all the holy days
             remain.
       Responding to his call
       a pleasant porter came,
       a watchman on the wall,
       who welcomed Sir Gawain.   810

'Good morning,' said our man. 'Will you bear a message
to the owner of this hall and ask him for shelter?'
'By St Peter,' said the porter, 'it'll be my pleasure,
and I'm willing to bet you'll be welcome to a bed.'
Then he went on his way, but came back at once
with a group who had gathered to greet the stranger;
the drawbridge came down and they crossed the ditch
and knelt in the frost in front of the knight
to welcome this man in a way deemed worthy.
820 Then they yielded to their guest, yanked open the gate,
and bidding them to rise he rode across the bridge.
He was assisted from the saddle by several men
and the strongest amongst them stabled his steed.
Then knights, and the squires of knights, drew near
to escort him, with courtesy, into the castle.
As he took off his helmet, many hasty hands
reached out to receive it and to serve this stranger,
and his sword and his shield were taken aside.
Then he made himself known to nobles and knights
830 and proud fellows pressed forward to confer their respects.
Still heavy with armour he was led to the hall
where a fire burned bright with the fiercest flames.
Then the master of the manor emerged from his chamber,
to greet him in the hall with all due honour,
saying, 'Behave in my house as your heart pleases.
To whatever you want you are welcome, do what
                    you will.'
              'My thanks,' Gawain exclaimed,
              'May Christ reward you well.'
840   Then firmly, like good friends
              they hugged and held a while.

Gawain gazed at the lord who greeted him so gracefully,
the great one who governed that grand estate,
powerful and large, in the prime of his life,
with a bushy beard as red as a beaver's,
steady in his stance, solid of build,
with a fiery face but with fine conversation;
a man quite capable, it occurred to Gawain,
of keeping such a castle and captaining his knights.
Escorted to his quarters the lord quickly orders   850
that a servant be assigned to assist Gawain,
and many were willing to wait on his word.
They brought him to a bedroom, beautifully furnished
with fine silken fabrics finished in gold
and curious coverlets lavishly quilted
in bloodless ermine and embroidered to each border.
Curtains ran on cords through red-gold rings,
tapestries from Toulouse and Turkistan
were fixed against walls and fitted underfoot.
With humorous banter Gawain was helped out   860
of his chain-mail coat and costly clothes,
then they rushed to bring him an array of robes
of the choicest cloth. He chose, and changed,
and as soon as he stood in that stunning gown
with its flowing skirts which suited his shape
it almost appeared to the persons present
that spring, with its spectrum of colours, had sprung;
so alive and lean were that young man's limbs
a nobler creature Christ had never created, they declared.
                    This knight,   870
          whose country was unclear,
          now seemed to them by sight
          a prince without a peer
          in fields where fierce men fight.

In front of a flaming fireside a chair
was pulled into place for Gawain, and padded
with covers and quilts all cleverly stitched,
then a cape was cast across the knight
of rich brown cloth with embroidered borders,
880 finished inside with the finest furs,
ermine, to be exact, and a hood which echoed it.
Resplendently dressed he settled in his seat;
as his limbs thawed, so his thoughts lightened.
Soon a table was set on sturdy trestles
covered entirely with a clean white cloth
and cruets of salt and silver spoons.
In a while he washed and went to his meal.
Staff came quickly and served him in style
with several soups all seasoned to taste,
890 double helpings as was fitting, and a feast of fish,
some baked in bread, some browned over flames,
some boiled or steamed, some stewed in spices
and subtle sauces to tantalize his tongue.
Four or five times he called it a feast,
and the courteous company happily cheered him
                    along:
          'On penance plates you dine –
          there's better board to come.'
          The warming, heady wine
900   then freed his mind for fun.

Now through tactful talk and tentative enquiry
polite questions are put to this prince;
he responds respectfully, and speaks of his journey
from the court of Arthur, King of Camelot,
royalty, and ruler of the Round Table,
and he says they now sit with Gawain himself,
who has come here at Christmastime quite by chance.
Once the master has gathered that his guest is Gawain
he thinks it so thrilling he laughs out loud.
All the men of that manor were of the same mind,   910
being keen and quick to appear in his presence,
this person famed for prowess and purity,
whose noble skills were sung to the skies,
whose life was the stuff of legend and lore.
Then knight spoke softly to knight, saying,
'Watch now, we'll witness his graceful ways,
hear the faultless phrasing of flawless speech;
if we listen we will learn the merits of language
since we have in our hall a man of high honour.
Ours is a generous and giving God   920
to grant that we welcome Gawain as our guest
as we sing of His birth who was born to save us.
                    We few
            shall learn a lesson here
            in tact and manners true,
            and hopefully we'll hear
            love's tender language too.'

Once dinner was done Gawain drew to his feet
and darkness neared as day became dusk.
930 Chaplains went off to the castle's chapels
to sound the bells hard, to signal the hour
of evensong, summoning each and every soul.
The lord goes alone, then his lady arrives,
concealing herself in a private pew.
Gawain attends too; tugged by his sleeve
he is steered to a seat, led by the lord
who greets Gawain by name as his guest.
No man in the world is more welcome, are his words.
For that he is thanked. And they hug there and then
940 and sit as a pair through the service in prayer.
Then she who desired to see this stranger
came from her closet with her sisterly crew.
She was fairest amongst them – her face, her flesh,
her complexion, her quality, her bearing, her body,
more glorious than Guinevere, or so Gawain thought,
and in the chancel of the church they exchanged courtesies.
She was hand in hand with a lady to her left,
someone altered by age, an ancient dame,
well respected, it seemed, by the servants at her side.
950 Those ladies were not the least bit alike:
one woman was young, one withered by years.
The body of the beauty seemed to bloom with blood,
the cheeks of the crone were wattled and slack.
One was clothed in a kerchief clustered with pearls
which shone like snow – snow on the slopes
of her upper breast and bright bare throat.
The other was noosed and knotted at the neck,
her chin enveloped in chalk-white veils,
her forehead fully enfolded in silk
960 with detailed designs at the edges and hems;

[46]

nothing bare, except for the black of her brows
and the eyes and nose and naked lips
which were chapped and bleared and a sorrowful sight.
A grand old mother, a matriarch she might
              be hailed.
        Her trunk was square and squat,
        her buttocks bulged and swelled.
        Most men would sooner squint
        at her whose hand she held.

Then Gawain glanced at the gracious-looking woman,
and by leave of the lord he approached those ladies
saluting the elder with a long, low bow,
holding the other for a moment in his arms,
kissing her respectfully and speaking with courtesy.
They request his acquaintance, and quickly he offers
to serve them unswervingly should they say the word.
They take him between them and talk as they walk
to a hearth full of heat, and hurriedly ask
for specially spiced cakes, which were speedily fetched,
980 and wine filled each goblet again and again.
Frequently the lord would leap to his feet
insisting that mirth and merriment be made:
hauling off his hood he hoisted it on a spear –
a prize, he promised, to the person providing
most comfort and cheer at Christmas time.
'And my fellows and friends shall help in my fight
to see that it hangs from no head but my own.'
So the laughter of that lord lights up the room,
and Gawain and the gathering are gladdened by games
990   till late.
                 So late, his lordship said,
                 that lamps should burn with light.
                 Then, blissful, bound for bed,
                 Sir Gawain waved goodnight.

So the morning dawns when man remembers
the day our redeemer was born to die,
and every house on earth is joyful for Lord Jesus.
Their day was no different, being a diary of delights:
banquets and buffets were beautifully cooked
and dutifully served to diners at the dais.   1000
The ancient elder sat highest at the table
with the lord, I believe, in the chair to her left;
the sweeter one and Gawain took seats in the centre
and were first at the feast to dine, then food
was carried around as custom decrees
and served to each man as his status deserved.
There was feasting, there was fun, and such feelings of joy
as could not be conveyed by quick description,
yet to tell it in detail would take too much time.
But I'm aware that Gawain and the beautiful woman   1010
found such comfort and closeness in each other's company
through warm exchanges of whispered words
and refined conversation free from foulness
that their pleasure surpassed all princely sports
                    by far.
            Beneath the din of drums
            men followed their affairs,
            and trumpets thrilled and thrummed
            as those two tended theirs.

They drank and danced all day and the next
and danced and drank the day after that,
then St John's Day passed with a gentler joy
as the Christmas feasting came to a close.
Guests were to go in the greyness of dawn,
so they laughed and dined as the dusk darkened,
swaying and swirling to music and song.
Then at last, in the lateness, they upped and left
towards distant parts along different paths.
Gawain offered his goodbyes, but was ushered by his host
to his host's own chamber and the heat of its chimney,
waylaid by the lord so the lord might thank him
profoundly and profusely for the favour he had shown
in honouring his house at that hallowed season
and lighting every corner of the castle with his character.
'For as long as I live my life shall be better
that Gawain was my guest at God's own feast.'
'By God,' said Gawain, 'but the gratitude goes to you.
May the High King of Heaven repay your honour.
Your requests are now this knight's commands.
I am bound by your bidding, no boon is too high
        to say.'
            At length his lordship tried
            to get his guest to stay.
            But proud Gawain replied
            he must now make his way.

[50]

Then the lord, being curious, made a courteous inquiry
of what desperate deed in the depth of winter
should coax him from Camelot, so quickly and alone,
before Christmas was over in his king's court.
'What you ask,' said the knight, 'you shall now know.   1050
A most pressing matter prised me from that place:
I myself am summoned to seek out a site
and I have not the faintest idea where to find it.
But find it I must by the first of the year, and not fail
for all the acres in England, so help me Lord.
And in speaking of my quest, I respectfully request
that you tell me, in truth, if you have heard the tale
of a green chapel, or the grounds where a green chapel stands,
or the guardian of those grounds who is coloured green.
For I am bound by a bond agreed by us both   1060
to link up with him there, should I live that long.
As dawn on New Year's Day draws near,
if God sees fit, I shall face that freak
more happily than I would the most wondrous wealth!
With your blessing, therefore, I must follow my feet.
In three short days my destiny is due,
and I would rather drop dead than default from duty.'
Then laughing out loud the lord said, 'Relax!
I'll direct you to your rendezvous when the time is right,
you'll get to the green chapel, so give up your grieving.   1070
You can bask in your bed, bide your time,
save your fond farewells till the first of the year
and still meet him by mid-morning to do as you may.
            So stay.
        A guide will get you there
        at dawn on New Year's Day.
        The place you need is near,
        two miles at most away.'

Then Gawain was giddy with gladness, and declared,
1080 'For this more than anything I thank you thoroughly.
Now my sight is set, and I'll stay in your service
until that time, attending every task.'
The lord squeezed Gawain's arm and seated him at his side,
and called for the ladies to keep them company.
There was pleasure aplenty in their private talk:
the lips of the lord ran wild with words,
like the mouth of a madman, not knowing his own mind.
Then speaking to Gawain, he suddenly shouted:
'You have sworn to serve me, whatever I instruct.
1090 Will you hold to that oath right here and now?'
'You may trust my tongue,' said Gawain, in truth,
'for within these walls I am servant to your will.'
The lord said warmly, 'You were weary and worn,
hollow with hunger, harrowed by tiredness,
yet you joined in my revelling right royally every night.
You relax as you like, lie in your bed
until Mass tomorrow, then go to your meal
where my wife will be waiting; she will sit at your side
to accompany and comfort you in my absence from court.
1100   So lounge:
                at dawn I'll rise and ride
                to hunt with horse and hound.'
                The gracious knight agreed
                and, bending low, he bowed.

'Furthermore,' said the master, 'let's make a pact.
Here's a wager: what I win in the woods will be yours,
and what you gain while I'm gone you will give to me.
Young sir, let's swap, and strike a bond,
let a bargain be a bargain, for worse or for better.'
'By God,' said Gawain, 'I agree to the terms   1110
and I find it pleasing that you favour such fun.'
'Let drink be served and we'll seal the deal,'
the lord cried loudly, and everyone laughed.
So they revelled and caroused uproariously,
those lords and ladies, for as long as they liked,
then they tired and they slowed and they stood and they spoke
with immaculate exchanges of manners and remarks.
And with parting kisses the party dispersed,
footmen going forward with flaring torches,
and every lord was led at last towards bed,   1120
               to dream.
         The houseguest and his host
         repeat their pact again.
         That lord knew more than most
         which tricks would entertain!

FITT III

Well before sunrise the servants were stirring;
the guests who were going had called for their grooms
and they scurried to the stables to ready the steeds,
trussing and tying all the trammel and tack.
The highest-ranking nobles got ready to ride,   1130
jumped stylishly to their saddles and seized the reins,
then cantered away on their chosen courses.
The lord of that land was by no means last
to be rigged out for riding with the rest of his men.
After mass he wolfed down a meal, then made
for the hunting grounds with his hunting horn.
So as morning was lifting its lamp to the land
his lordship and his huntsmen were high on horseback,
and the canny kennel-men had coupled the hounds
and opened the cages and called them out.   1140
On the bugles they blew three bellowing notes
to a din of baying and barking, and the dogs
which chased or wandered were chastened by whip.
As I heard it, we're talking a hundred top hunters
               at least.
        The handlers hold their hounds,
        the huntsmen's hounds run free.
        Each bugle blast rebounds
        between the trunks of trees.

1150 As the cry went up the wild creatures quaked.
 The deer in the dale, quivering with dread,
 hurtled to high ground, but were headed off
 by the ring of beaters who bawled and roared.
 The stags of the herd with their high-branched heads
 and the broad-horned bucks were allowed to pass by,
 for the lord of the land had laid down a law
 that man should not maim the male in close season.
 But the hinds were halted with hollers and whoops
 and the din drove the does to sprint for the dells.
1160 Then the eye can see that the air is all arrows:
 all across the forest they flashed and flickered,
 biting through hides with their broad heads.
 What! They bleat as they bleed and they die on the banks,
 and always the hounds are hard on their heels,
 and the hunters on horseback come hammering behind
 with stone-splitting cries, as if cliffs had collapsed.
 And those animals which escaped the aim of the archers
 were steered from the slopes down to rivers and streams
 and set upon and seized at the stations below.
1170 So perfect and practised were the men at their posts
 and so great were the greyhounds which grappled with the deer
 that prey was pounced on and dispatched with speed
    and force.
   The lord's heart leaps with life.
   Now on, now off his horse
   all day he hacks and drives.
   And dusk comes in due course.

So through a lime-leaf border the lord led the hunt,
while snug in his sheets lay slumbering Gawain,
dozing as the daylight dappled the walls,   1180
under a splendid cover, enclosed by curtains.
And while snoozing he heard a slyly made sound,
the sigh of a door swinging slowly aside.
From below the bedding he brings up his head
and lifts the corner of the curtain a little,
wondering warily what it might be.
It was she, the lady, looking her loveliest,
most quietly and craftily closing the door,
nearing the bed. The knight felt nervous;
lying back he assumed the shape of sleep   1190
as she stole towards him with silent steps,
then clasped the curtain and crept inside,
then sat down softly at the side of his bed.
And awaited him wakening for a good long while.
Gawain lay still, in his state of false sleep,
turning over in his mind what this matter might mean,
and where the lady's unlikely visit might lead.
Yet he said to himself, 'Instead of this stealth
I should ask openly what her actions imply.'
So he stirred and stretched, turned on his side,   1200
lifted his eyelids and, looking alarmed,
signed himself hurriedly with his hand, as if saving
                    his life.
          Her chin is pale, her cheeks
          are ruddy red with health;
          her smile is sweet, she speaks
          with lips which love to laugh:

'Good morning, Sir Gawain,' said the graceful lady.
'You sleep so soundly one might sidle in here.
You're tricked and you're trapped! But let's make a truce,
or I'll besiege you in your bed, and you'd better believe me.'
She giggled girlishly as she teased good Gawain.
The man in the bed said, 'Good morning, ma'am.
I'll contentedly attend whatever task you set,
and in serving your desires I shall seek your mercy,
which seems my best plan, in the circumstances!'
And he loaded his light-hearted words with laughter.
'But my gracious lady, if you grant me leave,
will you pardon this prisoner and prompt him to rise,
then I'll quit these covers and pull on my clothes,
and our words will flow more freely back and forth.'
'Not so, beautiful sir,' the sweet lady said.
'Bide in your bed – my own plan is better.
I'll tuck in your covers corner to corner,
then playfully parley with the man I have pinned.
Because I know your name – the knight Sir Gawain,
famed through the realm whichever road he rides,
whose princely honour is highly praised
amongst lords and ladies and everyone alive.
And right here you lie. And we are left all alone,
with my husband and his huntsmen away in the hills
and the servants snoring and my maids asleep
and the door to this bedroom barred with a bolt.
I have in my house an honoured guest
so I'll take my time; I'll be talking to him for
        a while.
    You're free to have my all,
    do with me what you will.
    I'll come just as you call
    and swear to serve you well.'

'In good faith,' said Gawain, 'such gracious flattery,
though in truth I'm not nearly such a noble knight.
I don't dare to receive the respect you describe
and in no way warrant such worthy words.
But by God, I'd be glad, if you give me the right,
to serve your desires, and with action or speech
bring you perfect pleasure. The honour would be priceless.'
Said the gracious lady, 'Sir Gawain, in good faith,
how improper on my part if I were to imply
any slur or slight on your status as a knight.   1250
But what lady in this land wouldn't latch the door,
wouldn't rather hold you as I do here –
in the company of your clever conversation,
forgetting all grief and engaging in joy –
than hug to her heart a hoard of gold?
I praise the Lord who upholds the high heavens,
for I have what I hoped for above all else by
                        his grace.'
            That lovely looking maid,
            she charmed him and she chased.   1260
            But every move she made
            he countered, case by case.

'Madam,' said our man, 'may Mary bless you,
in good faith, you are kind and the fairest of the fair.
Some fellows are praised for the feats they perform;
I hardly deserve to receive such respect,
whereas you are genuinely joyful and generous.'
'By Mary,' she declared, 'it's quite the contrary.
Were I the wealthiest woman in the world
1270   with priceless pearls in the palm of my hand
to bargain with and buy the best of all men,
then for all the signs you have shown me, sir,
of kindness, courtesy and exquisite looks –
a picture of perfection now proved to be true –
no person on this planet would be picked before you.'
'In fairness,' said Gawain, 'you found far better.
But I'm proud of the price you would pay from your purse,
and will swear to serve you as my sovereign for ever.
Let Christ now know that Gawain is your knight.'
1280   Then they muse on many things through morning and midday,
and the lady stares with a loving look,
but Gawain is a gentleman and remains on guard,
and although no woman could be warmer or more winning,
he is cool in his conduct, on account of the scene he
                 foresees:
          the strike he must receive,
          as cruel fate decrees.
          The lady begs her leave –
          at once Gawain agrees.

She glanced at him, laughed and gave her goodbye,   1290
then stood, and stunned him with astounding words:
'May the Lord repay you for your prize performance.
But I know that Gawain could never be your name.'
'But why not?' asked the knight, in need of an answer,
afraid that some fault in his manners had failed him.
The beautiful woman blessed him, then rebuked him:
'A good man like Gawain, so greatly regarded,
the embodiment of courtliness to the bones of his being,
could never have lingered so long with a lady
without craving a kiss, as politeness requires,   1300
or coaxing a kiss with his closing words.'
'Very well, 'said Gawain, 'let's do as you wish.
If a kiss is your request I shall keep my promise
faithfully to fulfil you, so ask no further.'
The lady comes close, cradles him in her arms,
leans nearer and nearer, then kisses the knight.
Then they courteously commend one another to Christ,
and without one more word the woman is away.
He leaps from where he lies at a heck of a lick,
calls for his chamberlain, chooses his clothes,   1310
makes himself ready then marches off to Mass.
Then he went to a meal which was made and waiting,
and was merry and amused till the moon had silvered
                    the view.
          No man felt more at home
          tucked in between those two,
          the cute one and the crone.
          Their gladness grew and grew.

And the lord of the land still led the hunt,
1320 driving hinds to their death through holts and heaths,
and by the setting of the sun had slaughtered so many
of the does and other deer that it beggared belief.
Then finally the folk came flocking to one spot
and quickly they collected and counted the kill.
Then the leading lords and their left-hand men
chose the finest deer – those fullest with fat –
and orderd them cut open by those skilled in the art.
They assessed and sized every slain creature
and even on the feeblest found two fingers' worth of fat.
1330 Through the sliced-open throat they seized the stomach
and the butchered innards were bound in a bundle.
Next they lopped off the legs and peeled back the pelt
and hooked out the bowels through the broken belly,
but carefully, being cautious not to cleave the knot.
Then they clasped the throat, and clinically they cut
the gullet from the windpipe, then garbaged the guts.
Then the shoulder blades were severed with sharp knives
and slotted through a slit so the hide stayed whole.
Then the beasts were prised apart at the breast,
1340 and they went to work on the gralloching again,
riving open the front as far as the hind-fork,
fetching out the offal, then with further purpose
filleting the ribs in the recognised fashion.
And the spine was subject to a similar process,
being pared to the haunch so it held as one piece
then hoisting it high and hacking it off.
And its name is the numbles, as far as I know, and
                         just that.
              Its hind legs prised apart
1350   they slit the fleshy flaps,
              then cleave and quickly start
              to break it down its back.

Then the heads and necks of hinds were hewn off,
and the choice meat of the flanks chopped away from the chine,
and a fee for the crows was cast into the copse.
Then each side was skewered, stabbed through the ribs
and heaved up high, hung by its hocks,
and every person was paid with appropriate portions.
Using pelts for plates, the dogs pogged out
on liver and lights and stomach linings   1360
and a blended sop of blood and bread.
The kill-horn was blown and the bloodhounds bayed.
Then hauling their meat they headed for home,
sounding howling wails on their hunting horns,
and as daylight died they had covered the distance
and were back in the abode where Gawain sat biding
                    his time.
          Warm friends, warm flames will meet
          the huntsman's home return.
          Gawain as well will greet   1370
          his host. Bright hearth-fires burn.

Then the whole of the household was ordered to the hall,
and the women as well with their maids in waiting.
And once assembled he instructs the servants
that the venison be revealed in view of the crowd,
and in excellent humour he hollered for Gawain
to see for himself the size of the kill,
and showed him the side-slabs sliced from the ribs.
'Are you pleased with this pile? Have I won your praise?
1380   Does my skill at this sport deserve your esteem?'
'Why yes,' said the other. 'It's the hugest haul
I have seen, out of season, for several years.'
'And I give it all to you, Gawain,' said the master,
'for according to our contract it is yours to claim.'
'Just so,' said Gawain, 'and I'll say the same,
for whatever I've won within these walls
such gains will be graciously given to you.'
So he held out his arms and hugged the lord
and kissed him in the kindliest way he could.
1390   'You're welcome to my winnings – to my one profit,
though I'd gladly have given you any greater prize.'
'I'm grateful,' said the lord, 'and Gawain, this gift
would carry more weight if you cared to confess
by what wit you won it. And when. And where.'
'That wasn't our pact,' he replied. 'So don't pry.
You'll be given nothing greater, the agreement we have
                    holds good!'
            They laugh aloud and trade
            wise words which match their mood.
1400   When supper's meal is made
            they dine on dainty food.

Later, they lounged by the lord's fire,
and were served unstintingly with subtle wines
and agreed to the game again next morning
and to play by the rules already in place:
any takings to be traded between the two men
at night when they met, no matter what the merchandise.
They concurred on this contract in front of the court,
and drank on the deal, and went on drinking
till late, when they took their leave at last,   1410
and every person present disappeared to bed.
By the third cackle of the crowing cock
the lord and his liegemen are leaping from their beds,
and Mass and the morning meal are taken,
and riders are rigged out ready to run as
                    day dawns.
          They leave the levels, loud
          with howling hunting horns.
          The huntsmen loose the hounds
          through thickets and through thorns.   1420

Soon they picked up a scent at the side of a swamp
and the hounds which first found it were urged ahead
by a wild-voiced hunter and his wailing words.
The pack responded with vigour and pace,
alert to the trail, forty lurchers at least.
Then such a raucous din rose up all around them
it ricocheted and rang through the rocky slopes.
The hounds were mushed with hollers and the horn,
then suddenly they swerved and swarmed together
1430   in a wood, between a pool and a precipice.
On a mound, near a cliff, on the margins of a marsh
where toppled stones lay scattered and strewn
they coursed towards their quarry with huntsmen close at heel.
Then a crew of them ringed the hillock and the cliff,
until they were certain that inside their circle
was the beast whose being the bloodhounds had sensed.
Then they riled the creature with their rowdy ruckus,
and suddenly he breaks the barrier of beaters –
the biggest of wild boars has bolted from his cover,
1440   ancient in years and estranged from the herd,
savage and strong, a most massive swine
with a fearsome grunt. And the group were disgruntled,
for three were thrown down by the first of his thrusts,
then he fled away fast before inflicting further damage.
The other huntsmen bawled 'hi' and 'hay, hay',
blasted on their bugles, blew to regroup,
so the dogs and the men made a merry din,
tracking him noisily, testing him time and time
                        again.
1450   The boar would stand at bay
                and aim to maul and maim
                the thronging dogs, and they
                would yelp and yowl in pain.

[68]

The front men stepped forward to fire a shot,
aimed arrows at him which were often on target,
but their points could not pierce his impenetrable shoulders
and bounced away from his bristly brow.
The smooth, slender shafts splintered into pieces,
and the heads glanced away from wherever they hit.
Battered and baited by such bombardment,   1460
in frenzied fury he flies at the men,
hurts them horribly as he hurtles past,
so that many grew timid and retreated a tad.
But the master of the manor gave chase on his mount,
the boldest of beast-hunters, his bugle blaring,
trumpeting the tally-ho and tearing through thickets
till the setting sun slipped from the western sky.
So the day was spent in pursuits of this style,
while our lovable young lord had not left his bed,
and, cosseted in costly quilted covers, there he   1470
                    remained.
            The lady, at first light,
            did not neglect Gawain,
            but went to wake the knight
            and meant to change his mind.

She approaches the curtains, parts them and peeps in,
at which Sir Gawain makes her welcome at once,
and with prompt speech she replies to the prince,
settling by his side and giggling sweetly,
1480 looking at him lovingly before launching her words.
'If this is Gawain who greets me, I am galled
that a man so dedicated to doing his duty
cannot heed the first rule of honourable behaviour,
which has entered through one ear and exited the other;
you have already lost what yesterday you learned
in the truest lesson my tongue could teach.'
'What lesson?' asked the knight. 'I know of none,
though if discourtesy has occurred then correct me, of course.'
'I encouraged you to kiss,' the lady said kindly,
1490 'and to claim one quickly when one is required,
an act which ennobles any knight worth the name.'
'Dear lady,' said the other, 'don't think such a thing,
I dare not kiss in case I am declined.
If refused, I'd be at fault for offering in the first place.'
'In truth,' she told him, 'you cannot be turned down.
If someone were so snooty as to snub your advance,
a man like you has the means of his muscles.'
'Yes, by God,' said Gawain. 'What you say holds good.
But such heavy handedness is frowned on in my homeland,
1500 and so is any gift not given with grace.
What kiss you request I will courteously supply,
have what you want or hold off, whichever
            the case.'
        So bending from above
        the fair one kissed his face.
        The two then talk of love:
        its grief; also its grace.

'I would like to learn,' said the noble lady,
'and please find no offence, but how can it follow
that a lord so lively and young in years,   1510
a champion in chivalry across the country –
and in chivalry, the chiefmost aspect to choose,
as all knights acknowledge, is loyalty in love,
for when tales of truthful knights are told
in both title and text the topic they describe
is how lords have laid down their lives for love,
endured for many days love's dreadful ordeal,
then vented their feelings with avenging valour
by bringing great bliss to a lady's bedroom –
and you the most notable of all noble knights,   1520
whose fame goes before him . . . yes, how can it follow
that twice I have taken this seat at your side
yet you have not spoken the smallest syllable
which belongs to love or anything like it.
A knight so courteous and considerate in his service
really ought to be eager to offer this pupil
some lessons in love, and to lead by example.
Is he actually ignorant, this man of eminence,
or does he deem me too dunce-like to hear of dalliances?
                    I come   1530
            to learn of love and more,
            a lady all alone.
            Perform for me before
            my husband heads for home.'

'In faith,' said Gawain, 'may God grant you fortune.
It gives me great gladness and seems a good game
that a woman so worthy should want to come here
and be happy and good-hearted with a humble knight
unfit for her favours – I am flattered indeed.
1540   But to take on the task of explaining true love
or touch on the topics those love-tales tell of,
with yourself, who I sense has more insight and skill
in the art than I have, or even a hundred
of the likes of me, however long we live,
would be somewhat presumptuous, I have to say.
But to the best of my ability I'll do your bidding,
bound as I am to honour you for ever
and to serve you as long as our Saviour preserves me!'
So the lady tempted and teased him, trying
1550   to enmesh him in whatever mischief she had in mind.
But fairly and without fault he defended himself,
no evil in either of them, only ecstasy
                    that day.
            At length, when they had laughed,
            the woman kissed Gawain.
            Politely then she left
            and went her own sweet way.

Roused and risen he was ready for Mass.
The meal of the morning was made and served,
then he loitered with the ladies the length of the day   1560
while the lord of the land ranged left and right
in pursuit of that pig which stampeded through the uplands,
breaking his best hounds with its back-snapping bite
when it stood embattled . . . then bowmen would strike,
goading it to gallop into open ground
where the air was alive with the huntsmen's arrows.
That boar made the best men flinch and bolt,
till at last his legs were like lead beneath him,
and he hobbled away to hunker in a hole
by a stony rise at the side of a stream.   1570
With the bank at his back he scrapes and burrows,
frothing and foaming foully at the mouth,
whetting his white tusks. The hunters waited,
irked by the effort of aiming from afar
but daunted by the danger of daring to venture
                    too near.
          So many men before
          had fallen prey. They feared
          that fierce and frenzied boar
          whose tusks could slash and tear.   1580

Till his lordship hacks up, urging on his horse,
spots the swine at standstill encircled by men,
then handsomely dismounts and unhands his horse,
brandishes a bright sword and goes bounding onwards,
wades through the water to where the beast waits.
Aware that the man was wafting a weapon
the hog's hairs stood on end, and its howling grunt
made the fellows there fear for their master's fate.
Then the boar burst forward, bounded at the lord,
1590 so that beast and hunter both went bundling
into white water, and the swine came off worst,
because the moment they clashed the man found his mark,
knifing the boar's neck, nailing his prey,
hammering it to the hilt, bursting the hog's heart.
Screaming, it was swept downstream, almost slipping
              beneath.
          At least a hundred hounds
          latch on with tearing teeth.
          Then, dragged to drier ground,
1600   the dogs complete its death.

[74]

The kill was blown on many blaring bugles
and the unhurt hunters hollered and whooped.
The chief amongst them, in charge of the chase,
commanded the bloodhounds to bay at the boar,
then one who was wise in woodland ways
began carefully to cut and carve up the carcass.
First he hacks off its head and hoists it aloft,
then roughly rives it right along the spine;
he gouges out the guts and grills them over coals,
and blended with bread they are titbits for the bloodhounds.   1610
Next he fetches out the fillets of glimmering flesh
and retrieves the intestines in time-honoured style,
then the two sides are stitched together intact
and proudly displayed on a strong pole.
So with the swine swinging they swagger home,
bearing the boar's head before that huntsman
who had fought with his fists in the ford till the beast
                          was slain.
          The day then dragged, it seemed,
          before he found Gawain,   1620
          who comes when called, most keen
          to countenance the claim.

Now the lord is loud with words and laughter
and speaks excitedly when he sees Sir Gawain;
he calls for the ladies plus the company of the court
and he shows off the meat slabs and shares the story
of the hog's hulking hugeness, and the full horror
of the fight to the finish as it fled through the forest.
And Gawain is quick to compliment the conquest,
1630   praising it as proof of the lord's prowess,
for such prime pieces of perfect pork
and such sides of swine were a sight to be seen.
Then admiringly he handles the hog's great head,
feigning fear to flatter the master's feelings.
'Now, Gawain,' said the lord, 'I give you this game,
as our wager warranted, as well you remember.'
'Certainly,' said Sir Gawain. 'It shall be so.
And graciously I shall give you my gains in exchange.'
He catches him by the neck and courteously kisses him,
1640   then a second time kisses him in a similar style.
'Now we're even,' said Gawain, 'at this evening's end;
the clauses of our contract have been kept and you have what
               I owe.'
        'By Saint Giles,' the just lord says,
        'This knight's the best I know.
        By wagering this way
        his gains will grow and grow.'

Then the trestle-tables were swiftly assembled
and cast with fine cloths. A clear, living light
from the waxen torches awakened the walls.   1650
Places were set and supper was served,
and a din arose as they revelled in a ring
around the fire in the fireplace, and the feasting party
sang song after song, at supper and beyond,
both traditional ditties and carols of the day,
with as much amusement as a mouth could mention.
The young woman and Gawain sat together all the while.
And so loving was that lady towards the young lord,
with stolen glances and secret smiles
that it muddled his mind and sent him half mad,   1660
but to snub a noblewoman was not in his nature,
and though tongues might wag he returned her attention
            all night.
        Before his friends retire
        his lordship leads the knight,
        heads for his hearth and fire
        to linger by its light.

They supped and swapped stories, and spoke again
of the night to come next, which was New Year's Eve.
1670 Gawain pleaded politely to depart by morning,
so in two days' time he might honour his treaty.
But the lord was unswerving, insisting that he stayed:
'As an honest soul I swear on my heart,
you shall find the green chapel to finalise your affairs
long before dawn on New Year's Day.
So lie in your room and laze at your leisure
while I ride my estate, and, as our terms dictate,
we'll trade our trophies when the hunt returns.
I have tested you twice and found you truthful.
1680 But think tomorrow *third time throw best*.
Now, a lord can feel low whenever he likes,
so let's chase cheerfulness while we have the chance.'
So those gentlemen agreed that Gawain would stay,
and they took more drink, then by torchlight retired to
their beds.
Our man then sleeps, a most
reposed and peaceful rest.
As hunters must, his host
is up at dawn and dressed.

After Mass the master grabs a meal with his men   1690
and asks for his mount on that marvellous morning.
All those grooms engaged to go with their lord
were high on their horses before the hall gates.
The fields were dazzling, fixed with frost,
and the crown of sunrise rose scarlet and crimson,
scalding and scattering cloud from the sky.
At the fringe of the forest the dogs were set free
and the rumpus of the horns went ringing through the rocks.
They fall on the scent of a fox, and follow,
turning and twisting as they sniff out the trail.   1700
A young harrier yowls and a huntsman yells,
then the pack come rushing to pick up the reek,
running as a rabble along the right track.
The fox scurries ahead, they scamper behind,
and pursue him at speed when he comes within sight,
haranguing him with horrific ranting howls.
Now and then he doubles back through thorny thickets,
or halts and hearkens in the hem of a hedge,
until finally, by a hollow, he hurdles a fence,
and carefully he creeps by the edge of a copse,   1710
convinced that his cunning has conned those canines!
But unawares he wanders where they lie in wait,
where greyhounds are gathered together, a group
                    of three.
          He springs back with a start,
          then twists and turns and flees.
          With heavy, heaving heart
          he tracks towards the trees.

Such earthly elation, hearing those hounds
1720   as they massed to meet him, marauding together,
and they bayed bloodily at the sight of his being,
as if clustering cliffs had crashed to the ground.
Here he was ambushed by bushwhacking huntsmen
waiting with a welcome of wounding words;
there he was threatened and branded a thief,
and always the hounds allowed him no ease.
Often, in the open, the pack tried to pounce,
then that crafty Reynard would creep into cover.
So his lordship and his lords were merrily led
1730   in this manner through the mountains until mid-afternoon,
while our handsome hero snoozed contentedly at home,
kept from the cold of the morning by curtains.
But love would not let her ladyship sleep
and the fervour she felt in her heart would not fade.
She rose from her rest and rushed to his room
in a flowing robe that reached to the floor
and was finished inside with fine-trimmed furs.
Her head went unhooded, but heavenly gems
were entwined in her tresses in clusters of twenty.
1740   She wore nothing on her face; her neck was naked,
and her shoulders were bare to both back and breast.
She comes into his quarters and closes the door,
makes her way to the window and throws it open,
then sweet and swift is the speech she intends for
                    his ear.
            'Oh, sir, how can you sleep
            when morning comes so clear?'
            And though his dreams are deep
            he cannot help but hear.

Yes, he dozes in a daze, dreams and mutters
like a mournful man with his mind on dark matters –
how destiny might deal him a death-blow on the day
when he grapples with the giant in the green chapel;
of how the strike of the axe must be suffered without struggle.
But sensing her presence there he surfaces from sleep,
drags himself out of his dreams to address her.
Laughing warmly she walks towards him
and finds his face with the friendliest kiss.
In a worthy style he welcomes the woman
and seeing her so lovely and alluringly dressed,
every feature so faultless, her complexion so fine,
a passionate heat takes hold in his heart.
Speech tripped from their tongues and they traded smiles,
and a bond of friendship was forged there, all blissful
                    and bright.
          They talk with tenderness
          and pride, and yet their plight
          is perilous unless
          sweet Mary minds her knight.

1770 For that noble princess pushed him and pressed him,
nudged him ever nearer to a limit where he needed
to allow her love or impolitely reject it.
He was careful to be courteous and avoid uncouthness,
cautious that his conduct might be classed as sinful
and counted as betrayal by the keeper of the castle.
'I shall not succumb,' he swore to himself.
With affectionate laughter he fenced and deflected
all the loving phrases which leapt from her lips.
'You shall bear the blame,' said the beautiful one,
1780 'if you feel no love for the female you lie with,
and wound her, more than anyone on earth, to the heart.
Unless, of course, there is a lady in your life
to whom you are tied and so tightly attached
that you could not begin to break the bond.
So in honesty and trust now tell me the truth;
for the sake of all love, don't be secretive or speak
                    with guile.'
                    'You judge wrong, by Saint John,'
                    he said to her, and smiled.
1790   'There is no other one
                    and won't be for a while!'

'Those words,' said the woman, 'are the worst insult.
But I asked, and you answered, and now I ache.
Kiss me warmly and then I will walk in the world
in mourning like a lady who loved too much.'
Stooping and sighing she kisses him sweetly,
then withdraws from his side, saying as she stands,
'But before we part will you find me some small favour?
Will you give me some gift – a glove at least,
that might leaven my loss when we meet in my memory?'   1800
'Well it were,' said Gawain. 'I wish I had here
my most priceless possession as a present for your sweetness,
for over and over you deserve and are owed
the highest prize I could hope to offer.
But I would not wish on you a worthless token,
and it strikes me as unseemly that you should receive
nothing greater than a glove as a keepsake from Gawain.
I am here on an errand in an unknown land
without men bearing bags of beautiful gifts,
which I greatly regret through my regard for you;   1810
but man must live by his means, and neither mope
                    or moan.'
           The pretty one replies:
           'Nay, noble knight, you mean
           you'll pass to me no prize.
           No matter. Here is mine.'

She offers him a ring of rich, red gold,
and the stunning stone set upon it stood proud,
beaming and burning with the brightness of the sun;
1820   what wealth it was worth you can well imagine.
But he would not accept it, and said straight away,
'By God, no tokens will I take at this time;
I have nothing to give, so nothing will I gain.'
She insists he receives it but still he resists,
and swears, on his name as a knight, to say no.
Snubbed by his decision, she said to him then,
'You refuse my ring because you find it too fine,
and don't dare to be deeply indebted to me;
so I give you my girdle, a lesser thing to gain.'
1830   From around her body she unbuckled the belt
which tightened the tunic beneath her topcoat,
a green silk girdle trimmed with gold,
exquisitely edged and hemmed by hand.
And she sweetly beseeched Sir Gawain to receive it,
in spite of its slightness, and hoped he would accept.
But still he maintained he intended to take
neither gold nor girdle, until by God's grace
the challenge he had chosen was finally achieved.
'With apologies I pray you are not displeased,
1840   but I must firmly refuse you, no matter how flattered
                I am.
        For all your grace I owe
        a thousand thank-yous, ma'am.
        I shall through sun and snow
        remain your loyal man.'

'And now he sends back my silk,' the lady responded,
'so simple in itself, or so it appears,
so little and unlikely, worth nothing, or less.
But the knight who knew of the power knitted in it
would pay a high price to possess it, probably.   1850
For the body which is bound within this green belt,
as long as it is buckled robustly about him,
will be safe against those who seek to strike him,
and all the slyness on earth wouldn't see him slain.'
The man mulled it over, and it entered his mind
that this girdle being given could be just the job
to save him from the strike in his challenge at the chapel.
With luck, it might let him escape with his life.
So relenting at last he let her speak,
and promptly she pressed him to take the present,   1860
and he granted her wish, gave in with good grace,
though the woman begged him not to whisper a word
of this gift to her husband, and Gawain agreed;
those words of theirs within those walls
                    should stay.
          His thanks are heartfelt, then.
          No sooner can he say
          how much it matters, when
          three kisses come his way.

Then the lady departed, leaving him alone,
for the man had amused her as much as he could.
And once she has quit he clothes himself quickly,
rises and dresses in the richest of robes,
stowing the love-lace safely aside,
hiding it away from all hands and eyes.
Then he went at once to the chapel of worship,
privately approached the priest and implored him
to allow his confession, and to lead him in life
so his soul might be saved when he goes to his grave.
Then fully and frankly he spoke of his sins,
no matter how small, always seeking mercy,
calling on that counsellor to clear his conscience.
The priest declares him so clean and so pure
that the Day of Doom could dawn in the morning.
Then in merrier mood he mingled with the ladies,
carolling and carousing and carrying on
like never before, until nightfall. Folk feel
and hear
and see his boundless bliss
and say, 'Such charm and cheer;
he's at his happiest
since his arrival here.'

And long let him loiter there, looked after by love.
Now the lord of the land was still leading his men,
finishing off the fox he had followed for so long.
He vaults a fence to flush out the victim,
hearing that the hounds are harrying hard.
Then Reynard scoots from a section of scrub
and the rabble of the pack rush right at his heels.
Aware of its presence the wary lord waits,   1900
then bares his bright sword and swishes at the beast,
which shirks from its sharpness, and would have shot away
but a hound flew forward before it could flee
and under the hooves of the horses they have him,
worrying their quarry with woeful wailing.
The lord hurtles from his horse and heaves the fox up,
wrestles it from the reach of those ravenous mouths,
holds it high over head and hurrahs manfully
while the bloodthirsty bloodhounds bay and howl.
And the other huntsmen hurried with their horns   1910
to catch sight of the slaughter and celebrate the kill.
And when the company of clansmen had come together
the buglers blew with one mighty blast,
and the others hallooed with open throats.
A human could not hear a headier music
than the roaring which was raised for the soul of Reynard
                who croaked!
            By way of a reward
            the hounds are soothed and stroked.
            Then red fur rips – Reynard   1920
            is cut out of his coat.

Then with night drawing near they headed homeward,
blaring their bugles with the fullness of their breath.
And at last the lord lands at his lovely home,
to find, by the heat of the fireside, his friend
the good Sir Gawain, in glad spirits
on account of the company he had kept with the ladies.
His blue robe flowed as far as the floor,
his soft-furred surcoat suited him well,
1930 and the hood which echoed it hung from his shoulders.
Both hood and coat were edged in ermine.
He meets the master in the middle of the room,
greets him graciously, with Gawain saying:
'I shall first fulfil our formal agreement
which we fixed in words when the drink flowed freely.'
He clasps him tight and kisses him three times
with as much emotion as a man could muster.
'By the Almighty,' said the master, 'you must have had luck
to profit such a prize – if the price was right.'
1940 'Oh fiddlesticks to the fee,' said the other fellow.
'As long as I have given the goods which I gained.'
'By Mary,' said the master, 'mine's a miserable match.
I've hunted for hours with nothing to my name
but this foul-stinking fox – fling its fur to the devil –
so poor in comparison with your priceless prizes,
these presents you impart, three kisses perfect
                    and true.'
            'Enough,' the knight entreats.
            'I thank you through and through.'
1950   The standing lord then speaks
            of how the fox-fur flew!

And with meals and mirth and minstrelsy
they made as much amusement as any mortal could,
and among those merry men and laughing ladies
Gawain and his host got giddy together;
only lunatics and drunkards could have looked more delirious.
Every person present performed party pieces
till the hour arrived when revellers must rest,
and the company in that court heard the call of their beds.
And lastly, in the hall, humbly to his host,   1960
our knight says goodnight and renews his gratitude.
'Your uncountable courtesies have kept me here
this Christmas – be honoured by the High King's kindness.
If it suits, I submit myself as your servant.
But tomorrow morning I must make a move;
if you will, as you promised, please appoint some person
to guide me, God willing, towards the green chapel,
where my destiny will dawn on New Year's Day.
'On my honour,' he replied. 'With hand on heart,
every promise I made shall be put into practice.'   1970
He assigns him a servant to steer his course,
to lead him through the land without losing time,
to ride the fastest route between forest
                    and fell.
          Gawain will warmly thank
          his host in terms that tell;
          towards the womenfolk
          the knight then waves farewell.

It's with a heavy heart that guests in the hall
1980   are kissed and thanked for their care and kindness,
and they respond with speeches of the same sort,
commending him to our Saviour with sorrowful sighs.
Then politely he leaves the lord and his household,
and to each person he passes he imparts his thanks
for taking such trouble in their service and assistance
and such attention to detail in attendance of duty.
And every guest is grieved at the prospect of his going,
as if honourable Gawain were one of their own.
By tapering torchlight he was taken to his room
1990   and brought to his bed to be at his rest.
But if our knight sleeps soundly I couldn't say,
for the matter in the morning might be muddying
                his thoughts.
         So let him lie and think,
         in sight of what he sought.
         In time I'll tell if tricks
         work out they way they ought.

FITT IV

Now night passes and New Year draws near,
drawing off darkness as our Deity decrees.
But wild-looking weather was about in the world: 2000
clouds decanted their cold rain earthwards;
the nithering north needled man's very nature;
creatures were scattered by the stinging sleet.
Then a whip-cracking wind comes whistling between hills
driving snow into deepening drifts in the dales.
Alert and listening, Gawain lies in his bed;
his lids are lowered but he sleeps very little
as each crow of the cock brings his destiny closer.
Before day had dawned he was up and dressed
for the room was livened by the light of a lamp.   2010
To suit him in his metal and to saddle his mount
he called for a servant, who came quickly,
bounded from his bedsheets bringing his garments.
He swathes Sir Gawain in glorious style,
first fastening clothes to fend off the frost,
then his armour, looked after all the while by the household:
the buffed and burnished stomach and breastplates,
and the rings of chain-mail, raked free of rust,
all gleaming good as new, for which he is grateful
               indeed.   2020
      With every polished piece
      no man shone more, it seemed
      from here to ancient Greece.
      He sent then for his steed.

He clothes himself in the costliest costume:
his coat with the brightly emblazoned badge
mounted on velvet; magical minerals
inside and set about it; embroidered seams;
a lining finished with fabulous furs . . .
2030 And he did not leave off the lady's lace girdle;
for his own good, Gawain won't forget that gift.
Then with his sword sheathed at his shapely hips
he bound himself twice about with the belt,
touchingly wrapped it around his waist.
That green silk girdle truly suited Sir Gawain
and went well with the rich red weaves that he wore.
But our man bore the belt not merely for its beauty,
or the appeal of its pennants, polished though they were,
or the gleam of its edges which glimmered with gold,
2040 but to save his skin when presenting himself,
without shield or sword, to the axe. To its swing
                    and thwack!
              Now he is geared and gowned
              he steps outside and thinks
              those nobles of renown
              are due his thorough thanks.

Then his great horse Gringolet was got up ready.
The steed had been stabled in comfort and safety
and snorted and stamped in readiness for the ride.
Gawain comes closer to examine his coat,   2050
saying soberly to himself, swearing on his word:
'There are folk in this castle who keep courtesy to the forefront;
let the man who hosts them find endless happiness.
And let his lady be loved for the rest of her life.
That he chose, out of charity, to cherish a guest,
showing kindness and care, then may heaven's King
reward him handsomely, and his household also.
For as long as I live in the lands of this world
I shall practise every means in my power to repay him.'
Then he steps in the stirrup and vaults to the saddle   2060
and his servant lifts his shield which he slings on his shoulder,
then he girds on Gringolet with his golden spurs
who clatters from the courtyard, not stalling to snort
                    or prance.
          His man was mounted too
          who lugged the spear and lance.
          'Christ keep this castle true,'
          he chanted. 'Grant good chance.'

The drawbridge was dropped, and the double-fronted gates
2070   were unbarred and each half was heaved wide open.
As he clears the planking he crosses himself quickly,
and praises the porter, who kneels before the prince
and prays that God be good to Gawain.
Then he went on his way with the one whose task
was to point out the road to that perilous place
where the knight would receive the slaughterman's strike.
They scrambled up bankings where branches were bare,
clambered up cliff-faces crazed by the cold.
The clouds which had climbed now cooled and dropped
2080   so the moors and the mountains were muzzy with mist
and every hill wore a hat of mizzle on its head.
The streams on the slopes seemed to fume and foam,
whitening the wayside with spume and spray.
They wandered onwards through the wildest woods
till the sun, at that season, came skyward, showing
        its hand.
    On hilly heights they ride,
    snow littering the land.
    The servant at his side
2090   then has them slow and stand.

'I have accompanied you across this countryside, my lord,
and now we are nearing the site you have named
and have steered and searched for with such singleness of mind.
But there's something I should like to share with you, sir,
because upon my life, you're a lord that I love,
so if you value your health you'll hear my advice:
the place you head for holds a hidden peril.
In that wilderness lives a wildman, the worst in the world,
he is brooding and brutal and loves bludgeoning humans.
He's more powerful than any person alive on this planet   2100
and four times the figure of any fighting knight
in King Arthur's castle, Hector included.
And it's at the green chapel where this grisliness goes on,
and to pass through that place unscathed is impossible,
for he deals out death blows by dint of his hands,
a man without measure who shows no mercy.
Be it chaplain or churl who rides by his church,
monk or priest, whatever man or person,
he loves murdering more than he loves his own life.
So I say, just as sure as you sit in your saddle,   2110
to find him is fatal, Gawain – that's a fact.
Trust me, he could trample you twenty times over

              or more.
       He's lurked about too long
       engaged in grief and gore.
       His hits are swift and strong –
       he'll fell you to the floor.'

'So banish that bogeyman to the back of your mind,
and for God's sake travel an alternative track,
ride another road, and be rescued by Christ.
I'll head off home, and with hand on heart
I shall swear by God and all his good saints,
and on all earthly holiness, and other such oaths,
that your secret is safe, and not a soul will know
that you fled in fear from the fellow I described.'
'Many thanks,' said Gawain, in a terse tone of voice,
'and for having my interests at heart, be lucky.
I'm certain such a secret would be silent in your keep.
But as faithful as you are, if I failed to find him
and lost my mettle in the manner you mentioned,
I'd be christened a coward, and could not be excused.
So I'll trek to the chapel and take my chances,
have it out with that ogre, speak openly to him,
whether fairness or foulness follows, however fate
                    behaves.
        He may be stout and stern
        and standing armed with stave,
        but those who strive to serve
        our Lord, our Lord will save.'

'By Mary,' said the servant, 'you seem to be saying   2140
you're hell-bent on heaping harm on yourself
and losing your life, so I'll delay you no longer.
Set your helmet on your head and your lance in your hand
and ride a route through that rocky ravine
till you're brought to the bottom of that foreboding valley,
then look towards a glade a little to the left
and you'll see in the clearing the site itself,
and the hulking superhuman who inhabits the place.
Now God bless and goodbye, brave Sir Gawain;
for all the wealth in the world I wouldn't walk with you   2150
or go further in this forest by a single footstep.'
With a wrench on the reins he reeled around
and heel-kicked the horse as hard as he could,
and was gone from Gawain, galloping hard
                    for home.
          'By Christ, I will not cry,'
          announced the knight, 'or groan.
          But find good fortune by
          the grace of God alone.'

2160 Then he presses ahead, picks up a path,
enters a steep-sided grove on his steed
then goes by and by to the bottom of a gorge
where he wonders and watches – it looks a wild place:
no sign of a settlement anywhere to be seen
but heady heights to both halves of the valley
and set with sabre-toothed stones of such sharpness
no cloud in the sky could escape unscratched.
He stalls and halts, holds the horse still,
glances side to side to glimpse the green chapel
2170 but sees no such thing, which he thinks is strange,
except at mid-distance what might be a mound,
a sort of bald knoll on the bank of a brook
where fell-water surged with frenzied force,
bursting with bubbles as if it had boiled.
He heels the horse, heads for that mound,
grounds himself gracefully and tethers Gringolet,
looping the reins to the limb of a lime.
Then he strides forward and circles the feature,
baffled as to what that bizarre hill could be:
2180 it had a hole at one end and at either side,
and its walls, matted with weeds and moss,
enclosed a cavity, like a kind of old cave
or crevice in the crag – it was all too unclear to
                    declare.
              'Green church?' chunters the knight.
              'More like the devil's lair
              where, at the nub of night,
              he makes his morning prayer.'

'For certain,' he says, 'this is a soulless spot,
a ghostly cathedral overgrown with grass,   2190
the kind of kirk where that camouflaged man
might deal in devilment and all things dark.
My five senses inform me that Satan himself
has tricked me in this tryst, intending to destroy me.
This is a haunted house – may it go to hell.
I never came across a church so cursed.'
With head helmeted and lance in hand
he scrambled to the skylight of that strange abyss.
Then he heard on the hillside, from behind a hard rock
and beyond the brook, a blood-chilling noise.   2200
What! It cannoned through the cliffs as if they might crack,
like the scream of a scythe being ground on a stone.
What! It whined and wailed, like a waterwheel.
What! It rasped and rang, raw on the ear.
'My God,' cried Gawain, 'That grinding is a greeting.
My arrival is honoured with the honing of an axe
                    up there.
          Then let the Lord decide.
          "Oh well" won't help me here.
          I might well lose my life   2210
          but freak sounds hold no fear.'

Then Gawain called as loudly as his lungs would allow,
'Who has power in this place to honour his pact?
Because good Gawain now walks on this ground.
Whoever will meet him should emerge this moment
and he needs to be fast – it's now or it's never.'
'Abide,' came a voice from above the bank.
'You'll cop what's coming to you quickly enough.'
Yet he went at his work, whetting the blade,
2220   not showing until it was sharpened and stropped.
Then out of the crags he comes through the cave-mouth,
whirling into view with a wondrous weapon,
a Danish-style axe for doling out death,
with a brute of a blade curving back to the haft
filed on a stone, a four-footer at least
by the look of the length of its shining lace.
And again he was green, like a year ago,
with green hair and flesh and a fully green face,
and firmly on green feet he came stomping forward,
2230   the handle of that axe like a staff in his hand.
At the edge of the water he will not wade
but vaults the stream with the shaft, and strides
with an ominous face onto earth covered over
            with snow.
        Our brave knight bowed, his head
        hung low – but not too low!
        'Young sir,' the green man said,
        'Your visit keeps your vow.'

The green knight spoke again, 'God guard you, Gawain.
Welcome to my world after all your wandering.   2240
You have timed your arrival like a true traveller
to begin this business which binds us together.
Last year, at this time, what was yielded became yours,
and with New Year come you are called to account.
We're very much alone, beyond view in this valley,
no person to part us – we can do as we please.
Pull your helmet from your head and take what you're owed.
Show no more struggle than I showed myself
when you severed my spine with a single smite.
'No,' said good Gawain, 'by my life-giving God,   2250
I won't gripe or begrudge the grimness to come,
so keep to one stroke and I'll stand stock still,
won't whisper a word of unwillingness, or one
                complaint.'
          He bowed to take the blade
          and bared his neck and nape,
          but, loath to look afraid,
          he feigned a fearless state.

Suddenly the green knight summons up his strength,
2260 hoists the axe high over Gawain's head,
lifts it aloft with every fibre of his life
and begins to bring home a bone-splitting blow.
Had he seen it through as thoroughly as threatened
the man beneath him would have met with his maker.
But glimpsing the axe at the edge of his eye
bringing death earthwards as it arced through the air,
and sensing its sharpness, Gawain shrank at the shoulders.
The swinging axe-man swerved from his stroke,
and reproached the young prince with piercing words:
2270 'Call yourself good Sir Gawain?' he goaded.
'Who faced down every foe in the field of battle
but now flinches with fear at the foretaste of harm?
Never have I known such a namby-pamby knight.
Did I budge or even blink when you aimed the axe,
or carp or quibble in King Arthur's castle,
or flap when my head went flying to my feet?
But entirely untouched, you are terror-struck.
I'll be found the better fellow, since you were so feeble
                    and frail.'
2280   Gawain confessed, 'I flinched
                 at first, but will not fail.
                 Though once my head's unhitched
                 it's off once and for all!'

'So be brisk with the blow, bring on the blade.
Deal me my destiny and do it out of hand,
and I'll stand the stroke without shiver or shudder
and be wasted by your weapon. You have my word.'
'Take this, then,' said the other, throwing up the axe,
menacing the young man with the gaze of a maniac.
Then he launches his swing but leaves him unscathed,   2290
withholds his arm before harm could be done.
And Gawain was motionless, never moved a muscle,
but stood stone-still, or as still as a tree stump
anchored in the earth by a hundred roots.
Then the warrior in green mocked Gawain again:
'Now you've plucked up your courage I'll dispatch you properly.
May the honourable knighthood heaped on you by Arthur –
if it proves to be powerful – protect your pretty neck.'
That insulting slur drew a spirited response:
'Get hacking, then, head-banger, your threats are hollow.   2300
Such huffing and fussing – you'll frighten your own heart.'
'By God,' said the green man, 'since you speak so grandly
there'll be no more shilly-shallying, I shall shatter you

       right now.'
       He stands to strike, a sneer
       from bottom lip to brow.
       Who'd fault Gawain if fear
       took hold? All hope is down.

Hoisted and aimed, the axe hurtled downwards,
2310   the blade bearing down on the knight's bare neck,
a ferocious blow, but far from being fatal
it skewed to one side, just skimming the skin
and finely snicking the fat of the flesh
so that bright red blood shot from body to earth.
Seeing it shining on the snowy ground
Gawain leapt forward a spear's length at least,
grabbed hold of his helmet and rammed it on his head,
brought his shield to his side with a shimmy of his shoulder,
then brandished his sword before blurting out brave words,
2320   because never since birth, as his mother's babe,
was he half as happy as here and now.
'Enough swiping, sir, you've swung your last swing.
I've borne one blow without bottling out,
go for me again and you'll get some by return,
with interest! Hit out, and be hit in an instant,
          and hard.
        One axe-attack – that's all.
        Now keep the covenant
        agreed in Arthur's hall
2330   and hold the axe in hand.'

The warrior steps away and leans on his weapon,
props the handle in the earth and slouches on the head
and studies how Gawain is standing his ground,
bold in his bearing, brave in his actions,
armed and ready. In his heart he admires him.
With volume but less violence in his voice, he replied
with reaching words which rippled and rang:
'Be a mite less feisty, fearless young fellow,
no insulting or heinous incident has happened
beyond the game we agreed on in the court of your king.   2340
One strike was promised – consider it served!
From any lingering loyalties you are hereby released.
Had I mustered all my muscles into one mega-blow
my axe would have dealt you your death, without doubt.
But my first strike fooled you – a feint, no less –
not fracturing your flesh, which was only fair
in keeping with the contract we declared that first night,
for with truthful behaviour you honoured my trust
and gave up your gains as a good man should.
Then I missed you once more, and this for the morning   2350
when you kissed my pretty wife then kindly kissed me.
So twice you were truthful, therefore twice I left
                    no scar.
          The person who repays
          will live to feel no fear.
          The third time, though, you strayed,
          and felt my blade therefore.'

'Because the belt you are bound with belongs to me;
it was woven by my wife so I know it very well.
And I know of your courtesies, and conduct, and kisses,
and the wooing of my wife – for it was all my work!
I sent her to test you – and in truth it turns out
you're by the far the most faultless fellow on earth.
As a pearl is more prized than a pea which is white,
so, by God, is Gawain, amongst gallant knights.
But a little thing more – it was loyalty that you lacked:
not because you're wicked, or a womaniser, or worse,
but you loved your own life; so I blame you less.'
Gawain stood speechless for what seemed like a century,
so shocked and ashamed that his stomach churned
and the fire of his blood brought flames to his face
and he wriggled and writhed at the other man's words.
Then he tried to talk, and finding his tongue, said:
'A curse upon cowardice and covetousness.
They breed villainy and vice, and destroy all virtue.'
Then he grabbed the girdle and ungathered its knot
and flung it in fury at the man in front.
'My downfall and undoing; let the devil take it.
Dread of the death-blow and cowardly doubts
meant I gave in to greed, and in doing so forgot
the fidelity and kindness which every knight knows.
As I feared, I am found to be flawed and false,
through treachery and untruth I have totally failed,' said

        Gawain.
      'Such terrible mistakes,
      and I shall bear the blame.
      But tell me what it takes
      to clear my clouded name.'

The green lord laughed, and leniently replied:
'The harm which you caused me is wholly healed.   2390
By confessing your failings you are free from fault
and have openly paid penance at the point of my axe.
I declare you purged, as polished and as pure
as the day you were born, without blemish or blame.
And this gold-hemmed girdle I present as a gift,
which is green like my gown. It's yours, Sir Gawain,
a reminder of our meeting when you mix and mingle
with princes and kings. And this keepsake will be proof
to all chivalrous knights of your challenge in this chapel.
But follow me home. New Year's far from finished –   2400
we'll resume our revelling with supper and song.
                    What's more
            my wife is waiting there
            who flummoxed you before.
            This time you'll have in her
            a friend and not a foe.

'Thank you,' said the other, taking helmet from head,
holding it in hand as he offered his thanks.
'But I've loitered long enough. The Lord bless your life
2410   and bestow on you such honour as you surely deserve.
And mind you commend me to your mannerly wife,
both to her and the other, those honourable ladies
who kidded me so cleverly with their cunning tricks.
But no wonder if a fool should fall for a female
and be wiped of his wits by womanly guile –
it's the way of the world. Adam fell for a woman
and Solomon for several, and as for Samson
Delilah was his downfall, and afterwards David
was bamboozled by Bathsheba and bore the grief.
2420   All wrecked and ruined by their wrongs; if only
we could love our ladies without believing their lies.
And those were fellows from fortunate families,
excellent beyond all others existing under heaven,'
                 he cried.
           'Yet all were charmed and changed
           by wily womankind.
           I suffered just the same,
           so clear me of my crime.'

'But the girdle,' he went on, 'God bless you for this gift.
Not for all its ore will I own it with honour,   2430
nor its silks and streamers, and not for the sake
of its wonderful workmanship or even its worth,
but as a sign of my sin – I'll see it as such
when I swagger in the saddle – a sad reminder
that the frailty of his flesh is man's biggest fault,
how the touch of filth taints his tender frame.
When my pulse races with passion and pride
one look at this love-lace will lessen my ardour.
But I will ask one thing, if it won't offend:
since I spent so long in your lordship's land   2440
and was hosted in your house – let Him reward you
who upholds the heavens and sits upon high –
will you make known your name? And I'll ask nothing else.'
'Then I'll treat you to the truth,' the other told him,
'Here in my homelands they call me Bertilak de Hautdesert.
And in my manor lives the mighty Morgan le Fay,
so adept and adroit in the dark arts,
who learned magic from Merlin – the master of mystery –
for in earlier times she was intimately entwined
with that knowledgeable man, as all you knights know   2450
            back home.
        Yes, "Morgan the Goddess" –
        I will announce her name.
        There is no nobleness
        she cannot take and tame.'

'She guided me in this guise to your great hall
to put pride on trial, and to test with this trick
what distinction and trust the Round Table deserves.
She imagined this mischief would muddle your minds
2460   and that grieving Guinevere would go to her grave
at the sight of a spectre making ghostly speeches
with his head in his hands before the high table.
So that ancient woman who inhabits my home
is also your aunt – Arthur's half-sister,
the daughter of the duchess of Tintagel; the duchess
who through Uther, was mother to Arthur, your king.
So I ask you again, come and greet your aunt
and make merry in my house; you're much loved there,
by me more than most, for as God be my maker
2470   your word holds more worth than most anyone in this world.'
But Gawain would not. No way would he go.
So they clasped and kissed and made kindly commendations
to the prince of paradise, and then parted in the cold,

           that pair.
       Our man, back on his mount
       now hurtles home from there.
       The green knight leaves his ground
       to wander who knows where.

So he winds through the wilds of the world once more,
Gawain on Gringolet, by the grace of God,   2480
under a roof sometimes and sometimes roughing it,
and in valleys and vales had adventures and victories
but time is too tight to tell how they went.
The nick to his neck was healed by now;
thereabouts he had bound the belt like a baldric –
slantwise, as a sash, from shoulder to side,
laced in a knot looped below his left arm,
a sign that his honour was stained by sin.
So safe and sound he sets foot in court,
and when clansmen had learned of their comrade's return   2490
happiness cannoned through the echoing halls.
The king kissed his kinsman and so did the queen,
and Gawain was embraced by his band of brothers,
who made eager enquiries, and he answered them all
with the tale of his trial and tribulations,
and the challenge at the chapel, and the great green chap,
and the love of the lady, which led to the belt.
And he showed them the scar at the side of his neck,
confirming his breach of faith, like a badge
                    of blame.   2500
          He grimaced with disgrace,
          he writhed in rage and pain.
          Blood flowed towards his face
          and showed his smarting shame.

'Regard,' said Gawain, grabbing the girdle,
'through this I suffered a scar to my skin –
for my loss of faith I was physically defaced;
what a coveting coward I became it would seem.
I was tainted by untruth and this, its token,
2510   I will drape across my chest till the day I die.
For man's crimes can be covered but never made clean;
once entwined with sin, man is twinned for all time.'
The king gave comfort, then laughter filled the castle
and in friendly accord the company of the court
allowed that each lord belonging to their Order –
every knight in the brotherhood – should bear such a belt,
a bright green belt worn obliquely to the body,
crosswise, like a sash, for the sake of this man.
So that slanting green stripe was adopted as their sign,
2520   and each knight who held it was honoured for ever,
as all meaningful writings on romance remind us;
an adventure which happened in the era of Arthur,
as the chronicles of this country have stated clearly.
Since fearless Brutus first set foot
on these shores, once the siege and assault at Troy
        had ceased,
      our coffers have been crammed
      with stories such as these.
      Now let our Lord, thorn-crowned,
2530   bring us to perfect peace. AMEN

HONY SOYT QUI MAL PENCE